Deer-Hair

Fly-Tying Guidebook

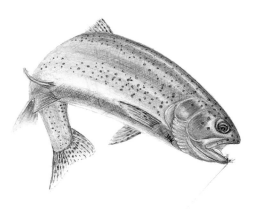

WRITTEN AND ILLUSTRATED BY

JACK PANGBURN

Deer-Hair
Fly-Tying Guidebook

WRITTEN AND ILLUSTRATED BY

JACK PANGBURN

Frank
Amato
PORTLAND

Acknowledgements

To Shirley,

My wife, partner and friend who has surprised me by being able to keep this book a secret; and to the many friends who have expressed words of encouragement just by asking the question, when are you going to do a book?

All inquiries should be addressed to:
Frank Amato Publications, Inc. • P.O. Box 82112 • Portland, Oregon 97282
503-653-8108 • www.amatobooks.com

Illustrations: Jack Pangburn
Fly Plate Photography: Jim Schollmeyer
Book Production: Tony Amato

SB ISBN: 1-57188-329-0 • SB UPC: 0-81127-00162-0
HB Ltd. ISBN: 1-57188-330-4 • HB Ltd. UPC: 0-81127-00163-7
Printed in Singapore

1 3 5 7 9 10 8 6 4 2

Contents

Introduction........7

Introduction

There are many ways to catch a fish, catching one on a fly you've tied yourself is by far the most exciting and rewarding. Many fly-anglers feel that tying the fly is as satisfying as netting the fish. There must be something to this because for thousands of years, anglers have been covering hooks with various materials that they think will look like something the fish would like in its diet. The methods of tying remain almost unchanged.

The purpose of this book is to explore and show you how to combine deer hair, the focus material, and other elements to create a finished fly. Since the hook is the skeleton or foundation on which the fly pattern is constructed that is where we will start. There are many hook manufacturers that in turn make many different hooks. The direction of the hook collection is to exhibit the hooks of one manufacturer and display the different hooks for the various types of flies, including streamers, nymphs, dry flies, wet flies and terrestrials.

A variety of materials are used to construct and form the anatomy of an artificial fly. The fantasy fly is based on something natural that a fish might eagerly eat, but does not necessarily have to look like a copy of the natural item.

The productive flies are so-called "searching" flies. These are tied to mimic and look in a general way like many food items that fish eat. Consideration of behavioral movement, size, form and color must all be computed and exhibited in the tied fly.

We know that most food items preyed upon by trout have natural earth-tone colors. There is no better way to imitate nature than to use what nature has to offer.

Of all the hair used in fly tying, that which belongs to the whitetail deer is the most popular and versatile. Deer hair from various parts of the deer body will be of different textures, length and color. These characteristics offer many opportunities for the fly tier to use the "focus material," *deer hair*, for many different purposes.

Chapter 1: *Primary Fly-Tying Materials*

Focus Material

The best uses of regional deer hair when fly tying:

Northern whitetail deer: Muddler-style spinning or flaring

Costal whitetail deer: Compara-duns size #10-16

Texas whitetail deer: Caddis and Humpies

Coues deer: Pale gray Compara-duns

Roe deer: Spinning Muddlers

Axis deer: Asian deer, farm raised, hair flares easily

Uses of deer hair from various parts of the deer body:

Mask: The face hair is short, fine texture, good for dubbing and is ideal for Compara-dun wings.

Back: Hair has varied texture, fairly long and is usually darker than the body hair.

Body: Hair is medium length, coarse to medium texture. Good for hoppers, Muddlers and other flies when floatability is wanted or needed.

Rump and Belly: The long coarse hair is ideal for spinning, and the white belly hair is excellent for dying different colors.

Legs: The short, fine-textured hair is best for small dry-fly wings, both upright and down, as well as parachute patterns, and also makes good dubbing hair.

Tail: The very long, coarse-textured hair is commonly called "bucktail" and is ideal for streamers of all kinds. The white hair also takes dye easily.

Bucktail: The whitetail's "flag" as it is usually called by deer hunters, has long, coarse hair that ends with fine hair tips and varies in color from black, dark brown to white. The longer hair of a deer's tail is ideal for bucktail streamers. The shorter hair is sometimes used for making dry-fly wings, parachutes and the high-floating Wulff patterns. The white hair, because it takes dye so well, provides the many different colors for use in tying the famous bucktail streamers.

Note: Deer-hair characteristics change as the seasons of the year change. The red phase in summer and gray phase in winter for northern deer. Warmer-climate deer (Texas) have fine-textured hair, not needing insulation from the cold, the hair is hollow only on the lower 1/3, but very variegated in brown and tan color values. The northern whitetail's body hair is pretty much hollow the full length, except for the fine tapered tips.

Primary Tying Materials

Whitetail body hair patch

Whitetail leg/hock hair piece

Whitetail "bucktail" piece

Mottled wild turkey wing quill and slip section

Peacock herl iridescent strands

Hackle (Note: Saddle hackle will work for most patterns in this book. Grizzly hackle with black and white bars and a red/brown hackle sometimes called Coachman brown are two basic hackle colors to have. A rust/orange ginger hackle and a furnace hackle of orange/brown color with a center strip of black would be your third and fourth hackles.)

Basic Materials

Hooks: Suggested Mustad hooks are described in Chapter 2

Weight: To weight the hook for the purpose of getting the fly to fish deeper in the water, lead-free wire is suggested. Try to match the hook diameter and use several wraps of the wire around the hook shank. Two useful sizes are .015 for hooks size 12-16 and .025 for hooks size 6-10.

Thread: Giorgio Benecchi 10/0 unwaxed is "super fine" and has breaking strength of 1lb.-6oz. Excellent for medium dry flies and nymphs, Chris Helm, of Whitetail Fly Tieing Supplies, guru of tying with deer hair claims, it also works great on caddis flies and other small deer-hair patterns. Go with a light gray dun color. A 100-meter spool costs about $2.60.

Gudebrod "G" is a thread that lays flat, is waxed and has a breaking strength of 3lb.-11oz. A very good thread choice for deer-hair tying and spinning where you need some tug. Choose gray again, 100-yard spool is about $1.50.

Dubbing: Various types of deer hair can be chopped, mixed or blended with other materials. It can also be used by itself and spun between two strands of waxed thread and then wrapped on the hook shank. Dubbing can be made from any other animal fur or hair, rabbit and squirrel work quite nicely.

SLF (Synthetic Living Fiber): A man-made product, some samples have iridescent colors in the mix. Suggested colors to have to use solo or blended with other materials including deer hair and feather fibers would be a yellow orange, olive green and dark brown.

Ribbing: A spool of gold wire, medium-size diameter .08 and a spool of gold oval tinsel, medium size. Spooled Mylar tinsel is gold on one side and silver on the other. The sizes indicate the width of the material. Fine for size 16-18, small for size 14, Medium for size 12 and large for size 10 fly hooks.

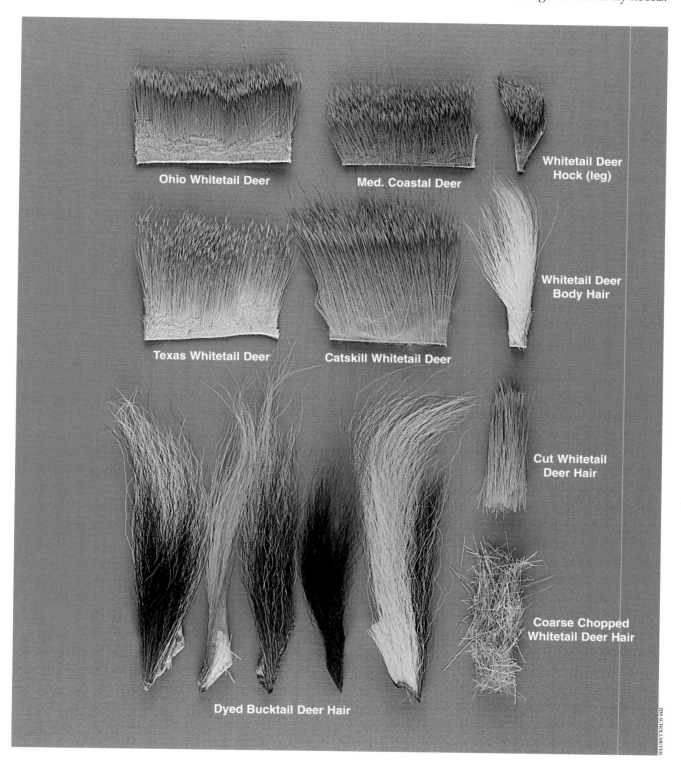

Ohio Whitetail Deer

Med. Coastal Deer

Whitetail Deer Hock (leg)

Texas Whitetail Deer

Catskill Whitetail Deer

Whitetail Deer Body Hair

Cut Whitetail Deer Hair

Coarse Chopped Whitetail Deer Hair

Dyed Bucktail Deer Hair

JIM SCHOLLMEYER

The Fly in the Art of Fly Fishing

Archaeologists believe man first discovered that feather-covered hooks could be very effective fishing equipment some time around 30,000 years ago in southern Europe. The hooks, which were eventually provided with barbs, were first made of bone and probably different woods.

In AD 200, the Roman Claudius Aelianus, in his book *On the Nature of Animals*, described how people fished with a fly in the river Astracus in Macedonia. The prey had a spotted exterior and is presumed to have been trout.

The Macedonians *"fastened red wool around a hook, and fixed onto the wool two feathers which grew under a cock's wattles, and which in colour are like wax. Their rod is six feet long, and their line is the same length. Then they throw their snare, and the fish, attracted and maddened by the colour, comes straight at it, thinking from the pretty sight to gain a dainty mouthful; when, however, it opens its jaws, it is caught by the hook."* These feather creations were more reminiscent of today's jigs than of flies, but we have no reason to doubt their fishing capability.

In the early 15th century, a manuscript, kept at the Bavarian abbey of Tegernsee, lists at least fifty different fly patterns for catching carp, pike, catfish, salmon along with trout and grayling. In the same century, Dame Juliana Berner in her *Book of St Albains, described fishing methods of the time in an article entitled "A Treatyse of Fysshynge Wyth an Angle."* This shows different hook patterns and that feather-attired hooks were also used as prey. Dame Juliana Berner is believed to have been the abbess of the Benedictine nunnery in Sopwell.

Her article, written in 1492 and subsequently hand-copied by monks until it was printed seventy years later, is absolutely decisive for the early development not only of fly-fishing but of sport fishing in general. It is the earliest known printed work in English on fly-fishing. It described in detail how fishing for trout and salmon was conducted with artificial flies. She had discovered, among other things, a seasonal regularity in the insects which she observed on her fishing waters. Her conclusion was that the fish's diet choice depended largely on the supply of swarming insects at the time. Her observations of insect life enabled her to develop twelve different fly patterns, one for each month. They are so well described that a fly tier today can tie them without much trouble.

Hooks

In order to build a house you need some sort of foundation. The hook is the foundation in fly tying, it is what every piece of material used gets fastened to. Just as with the many types of house foundations there are many hook foundation offerings, some radically different and some very similar depending on the function of the finished product.

Black Looper

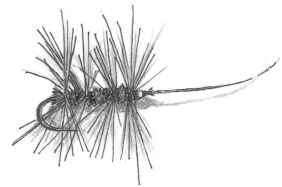

Dame Juliana Berner's fly #6 for the month of May, the Black Looper. The hook is barbless with a blind eye. The body is made of black wool and wrapped about with peacock tail (herl). The hackle is palmered brown capon (rooster) feathers.

Ruddy Fly

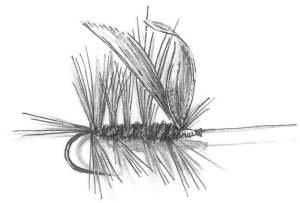

Dame Juliana Berner's fly #4 for the month of May, the Ruddy Fly. The hook is barbless and eyeless. The body is made or red wool wrapped barber-pole style with black silk. The wing feathers are from a drake (duck or goose). The palmered saddle hackle is from a red capon (rooster).

Where could deer hair be used as a substitute material on these two flies? Remember, the flies of this era were notably fished as wet flies.

See the Wiggle Damsel on a flex-jointed hook in the wrapping folder section.

For many fly tiers, hooks can be very confusing. There are many numbers, sizes and shapes, all of which can be useful at various times. All hooks have these features: point, bend, shank and an eye. The point is the end or tip, the bend is the curved part of the hook, the shank is the backbone of the hook and the eye is where you attach the line tippet or leader. Eyes can point in several directions, some point up, some down and some are straight. Down eyes are found on some dry flies and on most wet flies. The up eyes are commonly found on dry flies and on salmon hooks. Straight-eye hooks are mostly used on streamer hooks and saltwater hooks.

Hook length must be considered when designing your fly. The length will determine the fly's body length and in-turn the gap opening must offer enough room for hooking the fish. Some streamer hooks have a small gap space but the fly's body does not extend past a point directly above the hook point. This leaves the end of the hook open for business.

Mustad Hooks

The Mustad hooks illustrated will certainly do the job as indicated. Although Mustad offers many other special hook choices, I have limited the choices to the following list. When you look at the other hook manufacturers and what they offer it becomes a days job deciding what hook to use. I stick to the Mustad offerings, you may find you like the product of one of these hook makers: Gamakatsu, Tiemco, Daiichi, Partridge of Redditch, Gaelic etc.

HOOK SIZE CHART

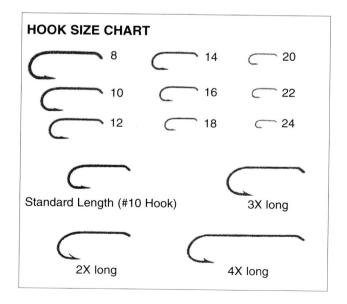

MUSTAD STREAMER-FLY HOOKS

Round bend, down eye, 3x long shank, sizes 6-16; use for extra-long nymphs, streamers, hoppers and stoneflies.

Round bend, down eye, 4x long shank, sizes 2-14; use for streamers and Woolly Buggers.

Limerick bend, down-looped eye, long shank, large sizes 4-10; use for Minnow streamers, Muddlers and Woolly Buggers.

MUSTAD DRY-FLY HOOK

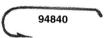

Standard dry-fly hook, round bend, down eye, fine (light) wire sizes 6-24; use for all floating flies.

MUSTAD WET-FLY HOOKS

Standard wet-fly hook, Sproat bend, down eye, sizes 6-20; use for all-around short wet flies and nymphs.

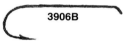

Wet-fly hook, 1x longer than 3906, Sproat bend, down eye, sizes 6-18; use for all-around long nymphs and wet flies.

MUSTAD CADDIS-FLY HOOK

Standard caddis hook, 1x short, straight eye, sizes 6-24; use for caddis pupae, larvae, and nymphs, sizes 6-16.

MUSTAD NYMPH-FLY HOOK

Curved-shank nymph hook, 3x long, straight eye, sizes 6-16; use for long burrower and swimmer nymphs and stonefly nymphs.

Stacking

Stack: A systematic pile, heap or bundle in a quantity; a number of things in one structure or collection; to pile up.

Streamers

There was a time, about 200 years ago, that a streamer was not considered a fly as it represented a small fish and not a flying insect. A fisherman who used a streamer was a streamer-fisherman and not a fly-fisherman. Over time, these views changed.

There are records of bucktail hairwing streamers being tied in America during the early 1870s, and offered for sale some 20 years later. A Maine fly tier, Herbert L. Welch, was credited as one of the first to use the longer-shank hook for streamer flies. Carrie G. Stevens, another Maine fly tier, is responsible for many streamer patterns still in use today, namely the Gray Ghost.

The British use the word "lure" to describe the type of fly we call a "streamer." Originally the word streamer meant a feather-winged pattern, the Gray Ghost as an example. About 75 years ago the bucktail hairwing patterns were introduced, meaning that the feather wing was replaced with natural or dyed bucktail hair.

The majority of small fish in moving waters are true bottom dwellers. This means that the fly fisherman's long shanked mimics of small fish should be fished as deep as possible. You can fish rather aggressively with the big streamer flies, fast or slow, upstream, across stream, and down stream. There are unlimited possibilities of variation, in contrast to the usual fishing with wet flies or nymphs.

Bucktail Streamers

Many of the most popular bucktail streamer patterns employ the use of a reflective silver body to imitate the silvery fish scales on the underbody of a baitfish. It is the hairwing colors that identify a particular bucktail streamer. A Mickey Finn is dressed in red and yellow. The black, brown and white bucktail wing portrays the Black-nose Dace. (See illustrations)

The sequence of steps when tying a bucktail or hairwing streamer are similar, only the stacking arrangement and the color of the hair being used will be different.

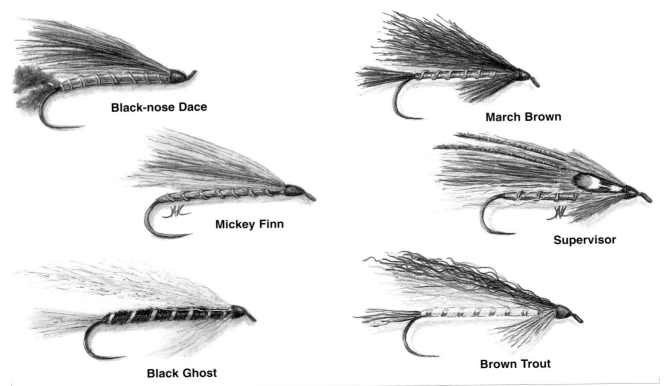

Black-nose Dace

Mickey Finn

Black Ghost

March Brown

Supervisor

Brown Trout

Black-nose Dace

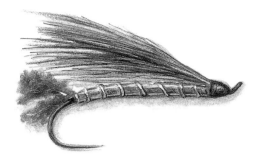

Hook: Streamer or long shank, size 6-10 (Mustad 9575)
Tail: Red poly yarn or floss
Underbody: For a more robust body, wrap the hook shank with a flat layer of dental floss
Body: Flat silver tinsel
Ribbing: Oval silver tinsel
Wing: White, brown or natural and black bucktail tied in stacked layers
Head: Smooth, glossy black finish.

TYING THE BLACK-NOSE DACE

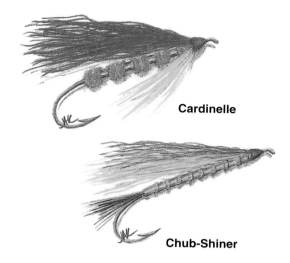

Cardinelle

Chub-Shiner

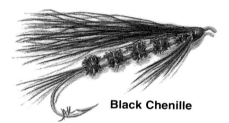

Black Chenille

Spooky Gray Ghost

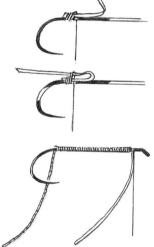

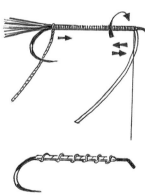

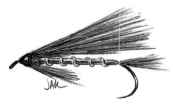

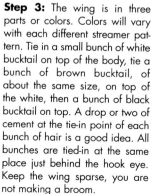

Step 1: Wrap tying thread down the hook to the bend. Tie in the tail material, only if required by the recipe. At the same place, tie in a length of oval silver tinsel or rib material. Return thread back up the hook shank and tie in a length of flat silver body tinsel near the hook eye.

Step 2: Develop the body by winding the flat tinsel down the hook and back again. Follow with the oval silver tinsel ribbing.

Step 3: The wing is in three parts or colors. Colors will vary with each different streamer pattern. Tie in a small bunch of white bucktail on top of the body, tie a bunch of brown bucktail, of about the same size, on top of the white, then a bunch of black bucktail on top. A drop or two of cement at the tie-in point of each bunch of hair is a good idea. All bunches are tied-in at the same place just behind the hook eye. Keep the wing sparse, you are not making a broom.

Step 4: Tie-off all bunches and form the thread head, apply several coats of cement. Coat with black enamel or lacquer until a smooth glossy finish is achieved.

Hairy Mary

Monroe's Killer

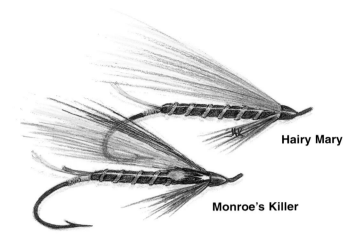

Hairy Mary

Monroe's Killer

Thread: Black
Tag: Gold tinsel
Tail: Golden pheasant crest
Body: Black floss or wool
Rib: Oval gold tinsel
Throat: Bright blue beard
Wing: Brown bucktail

Thread: Black
Tag: Oval silver tinsel and yellow floss
Tail: Golden pheasant crest topped by red hackle fibers
Body: Black floss
Rib: Fine oval silver tinsel
Throat: Blue guinea fowl
Wing: Orange bucktail topped with sparse yellow and black bucktail

The original Hairy Mary from the Highlands of Scotland was the template for most of the salmon hairwing wet flies. Compare the similarity of Munroe's Killer to the Hairy Mary. There are a great many Atlantic salmon wet-fly patterns that are constructed in the same manner. The variations are pronounced by changes in only the colors and sometimes the materials.

The Munro's Killer was first tied in Scotland, but modified patterns have been effective in Quebec's shore rivers and on rivers in New Brunswick. The Munro's Killer is claimed by the British to be one of the most popular hairwings in recent years. The American pattern illustrated shows some of the various garnishes we have given the dressing. We even spell its name differently, Monroe's as compared to Munro's.

BASIC TYING STEPS FOR HAIRWING PATTERNS

Step 1: Wind the thread around the hook shank to the bend of the hook and tie-in a cut length of oval gold tinsel for the tag and the rib. Return-wrap the thread to just short of the hook eye. Leave room for tying in beard and wing materials. Tie-in a length of floss. (Note that floss is easier to work with if dampened with water.)

Step 2: The body is formed by wrapping the floss the length of the hook shank and back. Tie-in and cut off the excess. Wrap three turns of oval gold tinsel around the top of the hook bend to form a gold tag; then rib the body with the remaining tinsel and remove surplus.

Step 3: Tie-in under the chin of the hook eye a few hackle fibers for a beard. On top of the hook tie in small bunches of bucktail above the beard. It is, easier to handle small bunches instead of trying to tie in the whole wing at one time. Finish with a neat thread head, add cement and varnish for durability.

Texas Jim Stonefly Streamer

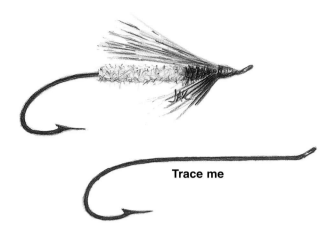

Trace me

Body: Rear 2/3, cream Antron or rabbit fur dubbing
Front 1/3 black Antron or rabbit fur dubbing
Hackle: Black hackle palmered forward over the black forward 1/3
Wing: Natural brown deer hair

Texas Jim Stonefly Streamer is a low-water style streamer with reduced or sparse dressing materials. This low-water pattern was created by outdoor writer and guide "Rocky" Schulstad of Newfoundland around 1965. The fly imitates a yellow stonefly common to the area's Serpentine River. While guiding Jim Barnett, the newspaper man, from Texas who had great success with the fly it was christened with his name Texas Jim. (Note the two illustrations; trace the bare hook and create your own hairwing fly variant.)

Stonefly Design

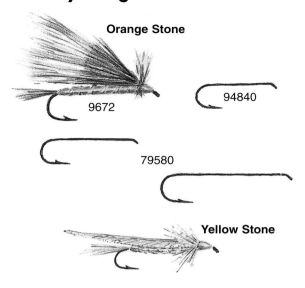

Orange Stone

9672

94840

79580

Yellow Stone

Little Yellow Stone

Thread: Yellow
Tail: Short tan deer hair
Body: Bundled deer hair dyed yellow
Rib: Yellow thread
Wings: Gray hackle tips
Hackle: Sparse gray dun
Head: Yellow thread

Brown Owl

Thread: Black
Underbody: Dental floss
Overbody: Oval gold tinsel
Rib: None
Wing: Grizzly hackle tips
Hackle: Sparse grizzly
Sight Target: Bonnet or hat of bright yellow Antron

Caddis

Caddis or sedges, as they are sometimes called, are the aquatic cousins to butterflies and moths. They go through the egg, larva, pupa and adult stages. It is basically recognized that trout like to feed on insects that are in transition stage from nymph to adult, called emergers. In a relative ranking of what trout eat, the caddis is the third most important food source. Nighttime feeding actually places the caddis as the second most important evening food source. Only scuds (shrimp) are more frequently consumed in the nighttime hours.

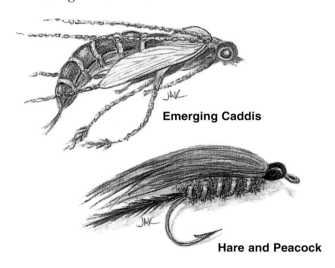

Emerging Caddis

Hare and Peacock

The emerging caddis does not have wings, but its legs are very apparent. If the legs are imitated by soft hackle or hair, they mimic the quivering natural movement that makes the soft-hackle fly so effective. Some of the old soft-hackle patterns include the Partridge and Green and Partridge and Orange, Breadcrust, and the Brown Hackle. The Hare and Peacock I improvised a few years ago has proven to be a good "go-to fly" for imitating emerging caddis. The word "hare" could be changed to "hair" and deer hair could be substituted for the rabbit fur.

Adult caddis are usually taken from the top of the water by trout while they are hatching and letting their wings dry, or when they return to the water for laying eggs to start the life cycle over again. The shades of color in deer hair are fairly descriptive of the coloration of caddis wings. Deer hair is an excellent material for tying flies to imitate adult caddis, and it floats.

Buck Caddis (A floating adult deer-hair caddis)

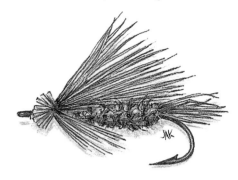

Hook: Long shank, size 4-12 (Mustad 79580)
Thread: Brown, gray or olive
Tail: Short brown deer hair from legs or face mask
Body: Floss, color of choice or chopped deer-hair dubbing
Rib: Gold tinsel cord, thread, floss or palmered hackle
Beard: Same as tail
Wing: Long natural tan deer body hair
Head: Trimmed wing butts

A very popular fly during the caddis hatches, usually tied in the brown, gray or olive colors. Fished as a caddis adult, the pattern can be tied in any color needed to match the naturals. Adding a palmered hackle along the length of the body permits the fly to float high in the water and is perfect for fishing fast water when necessary.

Stonefly

A long-shank hook pattern of an adult caddis fly will also be serviceable as an adult stonefly. However, the adult stonefly patterns are considered to be less important to the fly-fisherman. It's the stonefly nymphs that are definitely worth imitating. Again, a large size 6-12 deer-hair mayfly nymph gives a pretty good suggestion of a stonefly nymph. Think about this when you are tying flies. Limited patterns but in different sizes will cover most fishing situations such as a small-sized nymph for mayflies and a large nymph for stoneflies.

Mayfly - Stonefly Nymph

White Top
(A deer-hair adult caddis or stonefly pattern)

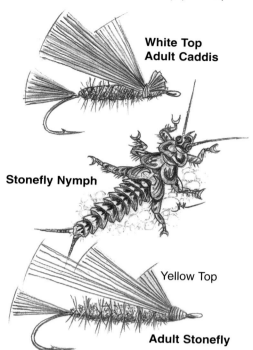

White Top Adult Caddis

Stonefly Nymph

Yellow Top

Adult Stonefly

Hook: For caddis, use a Mustad 94840 (dry) size 12-18; for a stonefly, use a Mustad 79580 (streamer) size 6-12
Thread: Black or gray
Body: Gray, olive or brown fur or deer-hair dubbing
Hackle rib: Grizzly or dark dun
Wing: Natural deer body hair over which is a top of white deer hair, yellow could be substituted for the white. It is a sight aid for the fisherman, not the fish.
Head: Wing butt ends trimmed at an angle.

Fluttering Orange Stonefly

Hook: 2x or 3x long shank, size 8 (Mustad 9672)
Thread: Orange
Tail: Short natural deer hair
Body: Orange Antron yarn or dubbing
Rib: Gold twist cord, green string or thread
Wing: White or light tan deer hair
Shawl or Shoulder: Short natural, dark deer hair
Hackle: Tan, cream or ginger

If you intend to tie an adult caddis in the method illustrated for a Fluttering Stonefly you need to downsize the hook, a Mustad 94840 dry-fly hook would be a good choice in sizes 10-16. Also, substitute an olive, gray or brown floss body for the stonefly's orange. As you will see, if you haven't already, a similar tying method of sequences can be used to tie many fly patterns.

THE TYING STEPS ARE VERY MUCH LIKE THE BUCKTAIL STREAMER SEQUENCES

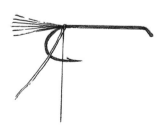

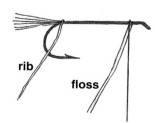

rib

floss

Step 1: At the end of the hook, tie in the tail. Next tie in a length of rib material.

Step2: Travel the tying thread back to just behind hook eye. Tie in a length of floss and wind floss from front to back and back to the front end of the hook to form the body.

Step 3: Palmer the rib material and remove excess. Attach a small bunch of light tan, natural deer hair on top of the hook for a wing. Top the wing with a shawl of shorter dark deer hair. Tie in a hackle and finish the head with thread and cement.

Clouser Minnow

This pattern is part of the stacking method that employs bunches of deer hair on top or back and on the bottom or belly with the hook sandwiched between the two stacked bunches. Bucktail hair is used to achieve the long body of a minnow. As noted before, white bucktail hair takes color dyes beautifully and provides the fly tier with many possible combinations. I refer to the many hairwing salmon flies and bucktail streamers for some of those combinations. This pattern has a unique characteristic, the fly is tied and weighted so that the hook will fish USD (up side down).

Clouser Deep Minnow

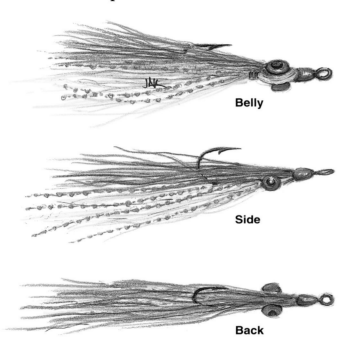

Belly

Side

Back

Bob Clouser, fly-tying instructor, fly shop owner and fishing guide, is the one responsible for the design of this fly that has caught many species of fish in both salt and fresh water. I had the very good fortune, a few years back, to take a tying class taught by the originator of the Clouser Minnow. Bob walked us through the steps with first-rate instruction. We tied both the fresh- and saltwater versions of his upside down minnow pattern, as well as his bass popper surface fly.

Clouser Deep Minnow

Hook: Large 1/0 down to a size 2, 4, or 6. The hook is placed in the vise with the hook point down. Dumbbell eyes are tied on top of the hook a distance back from the hook eye.

Eyes: Lead dumbbell style painted red with a black pupil.

Beard or Belly: Orange and yellow bucktail is tied in behind the hook eye and again behind the dumbbell eye with the long hair extending a hook length beyond the hook bend. Krystal Flash is usually added to the bunch of bucktail.

Note: The hook is now removed turned up side down and replaced back in the vise jaws. If you have a rotating vise, it's a simple task to turn the hook up side down.

Wing or Back: Tie on the red bucktail with some copper-colored Krystal Flash just behind the hook eye. This bunch of red bucktail should extend at least the length of the belly bunch and a little beyond if possible.

Head: Thread head of the same color as the back.

The freshwater pattern is tied in the same sequence, only using a smaller hook and changing the belly color to white, the back color to a green brown mix and painting smaller dumbbell eyes yellow or orange with a black pupil.

Thunder Creek Streamers

The Thunder Creek streamers were introduced by Keith Fulsher in the early 1970's. His new flies represented years of studying the baitfish minnows and how to accurately imitate them. Fulsher was not the first to work with reverse-wing bucktails. Carrie Stevens of Ghost Streamers fame tried the reverse-wing minnows but never perfected them to the point that Fulsher did with his slim, streamlined baitfish imitations. Thunder Creek flies have been found to be more effective when tied very sparse.

Golden Shiner

Hook: Long-shank streamer type, size 6-12 (Mustad 79580 or 9672)
Thread: White
Body: Pearlescent Mylar tubing
Throat and Belly: White bucktail
Wings or Sides: Cream or tan bucktail
Back: Olive bucktail
Neck or Gills: Red paint or red thread
Eyes: Yellow or orange with black pupils

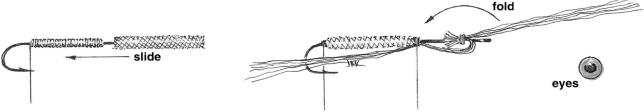

Step 1: Start with covering the hook shank with a couple layers of thread wraps as an underbody. The woven Mylar tube is expandable; *slide* one end over the hook eye and tie the leading end to the top of the hook bend. A touch of head cement at this point will keep the Mylar tube from traveling or coming apart.

Step 2: Attach the bucktail as illustrated and *fold* back toward the hook bend. Again some cement on the butt ends of the tied-in bucktail is a good idea.

Step 3: The back, sides (wings) and belly are tied on in separate sparse bunches. The belly bunch is usually white, the sides are a medium color value and the back is of a darker value. The neck or gills are painted red or wrapped with red thread.

Step 4: The eyes are painted on by using two dowel rods, one of eyeball-size diameter, the other pupil size. Dip the end of the larger dowel in some yellow or orange paint and stamp an eyeball on each side of the fly head. When the paint is dry repeat the stamping, this time using the smaller dowel and black paint for the pupils.

Chapter 4: *Wrapping*

Wrap: To bind, encase or close. In terms of fly-tying, it's the cover-wrapping on the hook that is the first step in most fly-tying sequence. The simple flies described in this section would be nothing but naked hooks without the wrap or the wrapping procedure.

Green Rock Worm

 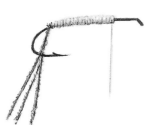 

Step 1: At the hook bend, tie in 3 or 4 long strands of bucktail, dyed fluorescent green and 2 or 3 full strands of peacock herl.

Step 2: Wrap the hook shank with tight side-by-side wraps of the bucktail. (Note if the bucktail is dampened with water before wrapping, it is easier to use and behaves quite well.)

Step: 3 Twist the 2 or 3 strands of peacock herl together and palmer a rib the length of the green body; at the thorax, make a thick collar by wrapping a couple times. Secure the herl and collar with fluorescent green thread and construct a small thread head.

Note: For fly durability, because the peacock herl is fragile, coat the entire fly with head cement.

The use of weight is optional but this fly should be fished on the bottom; lead wire wrapped on the hook shank, a bead head behind the hook eye or shot added to the leader system are all possibilities.

You may want to use lead-free weight materials, lead is a no-no in some waters.

The Red Blood Worm would be constructed the same way as the Green Rock Worm. The exception, of course, would be the color of the bucktail hair strands.

Rock Worm Larva

This is a caddis larva pattern. If tied on a very small hook, it can also represent a midge drifting in the water's surface film. However, caddis larvae live on the bottom and move only slowly. When fishing on the bottom, retrieve the fly smoothly at about a half inch per second. Pause once in a while during the retrieve.

Rock Worm Larva

Hook: Long-shank curve Mustad 80050BR, size 14-16 for bottom-dwelling caddis larvae. For midge larvae hanging in the film, use a light-weight dry-fly hook, like Mustad 94840 size 18-24. The deer-hair collar will aid in floatation

Weight: Optional addition of lead wire wraps on the hook to be used for bottom-dwelling larvae

Thread: Color of bucktail used for the body

Body: Wrapped with dyed bucktail of fluorescent green, brown, olive or mustard

Rib: Thread palmered for segmentation

Hackle: Spun natural color deer hair

Yellow Wet Fly Pupa

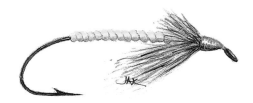

Hook: Nymph size 10-16
Thread: Yellow-brown mustard color
Abdomen: Wrap hook shank with bucktail dyed yellow-brown
Thorax: Soft brown upland gamebird hackle. Finish with small head.

The Bundled Body fly and procedure is included here because of the wrapping transition of thread used on an extended fly body. This time the tier is wrapping a bundle of bucktail by itself or with a hook shank inside. The section on Bundling will give more details on the flies made in this manner.

Bundled Body

The fly illustrated has an extended abdomen with a few loose strands of bucktail for legs. This pattern as is will imitate a swimming damselfly nymph. Put a bend in the hook before tying; a bend to the left or right side in the hook shank produces some erratic movement to the fly in the water. Follow the tying steps indicated for the fly above. Also the extended body directions in Chapter 10 on page 47, "Bundled Bodies".

Damselfly Nymph

Damselfly Nymph

The somewhat-buoyant deer hair and the weight of the hook, combined with the deer-hair thorax allows this fly pattern to hang at or just under the surface of the water. A damselfly nymph is pretty good sized compared to midges and the smaller mayfly nymphs, making it good fare for trout.

The Wiggle Damsel has a jointed fly body using a monofilament loop wrapped on the hook shank with some epoxy glue applied in the wrap area. This loop hinge allows the abdomen to wiggle up and down and from side to side while the thorax is pulled through the water. The trailing hook bend is cut off and the shank is attached via the eye to the mono loop on the lead hook. The trailing hook must obviously be attached before the mono loop is closed and wrapped with thread.

Wiggle Damsel

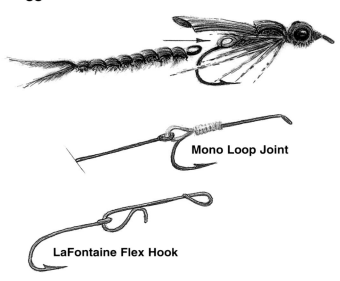

Mono Loop Joint

LaFontaine Flex Hook

Hook: A mono loop joint or a flex-hook arrangement developed by Gary LaFontaine. His hook system allows the two hooks to be tied separately and joined together when ready for completion.
Thread: Olive
Tail: Peacock or hackle tips
Abdomen: Trailing hook body, twisted deer-hair dubbing
Back: Pheasant tail section
Rib: Copper wire
Thorax: Lead hook
Body: Twisted deer-hair dubbing
Legs: Hackle fibers
Eyes: Black plastic dumbbell type
Back: Mottled turkey wing section
Rib: Copper wire
Head: Body dubbing and thread wrapped

Shrimp

The Pink Flash saltwater shrimp fly is another example of a wrapping pattern. The Pink Flash fly is shown in illustration as a USD, an up-side-down bottom-hugging wet-fly pattern. The shrimp has many abdominal moving appendages, the deer-hair wing offers duplication of their movement. Shrimp, like crabs, swim backwards with strokes of their fantail and crawl forward. This movement is in opposition to the illustrated fly patterns, maybe the eyes and head should be on the bend of the hook. However, the fish do not seem to mind the juxtaposition.

Pink Flash (USD Saltwater)

Hook: Saltwater hooks are generally blackened or stainless
Weight: Lead wire wraps, or if lead dumbell eyes are used the lead wire is overkill.
Underbody: Cocoon the hook with dental floss to build body bulk
Eyes: Bead chain painted red if wire weight is used, lead dumbell eyes if not
Overbody: Bucktail dyed pink wrapped over underbody
Wing: Light pink, gray or white deer hair or bucktail depending on hook size

The yellow-orange shrimp pattern offers the option of omitting the eyes or painting eyes on the epoxy head

Fluorescent Grub

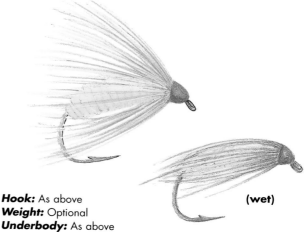

(wet)

Hook: As above
Weight: Optional
Underbody: As above
Body: Yellow chenille wrapped full
Rib: Orange thread
Collar: Spun fluorescent yellow and orange dyed deer hair
Head: Soft body epoxy, painted red

This illustration does not have much to do with the use of deer hair, but the procedure options will serve well when building horizontal hackles on wrapped and bundled bodies. The sequence works equally as well on dubbed bodies.

Gallows Loop

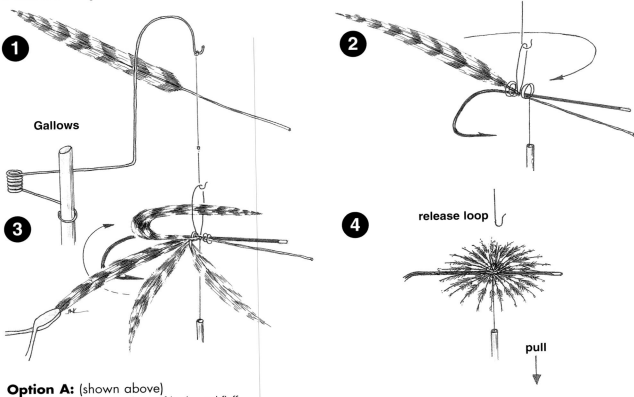

Option A: (shown above)
Step 1: Strip hackle stem base of barbs and fluff.
Step 2: Loop the stem to the hook, as in Drawing 2, two to three wraps held by bobbin weight. Do not make too many loops or pull thread tight because stem has to slide under wraps in the locking-down process.
Step 3: Connect the gallows, an engineered mild tension spring wire hook, to the thread loop, Drawing 3. Wrap the hackle around the loop base for the desired number of turns. Pull the hackle tip through the loop, remove the gallows hook, hold the hackle tip and pull the thread down to close the loop, Drawing 4, and lock down the hackle in a way similar to whip finishing.

Option B:
Tie on two grizzly hackles so the stems or butt ends are standing up at a right angle to the hook shank. Use the stems as a post for the horizontal parachute hackle that will settle down flush on the water's surface. Of course the remaining hackle is used to wrap around the post to create the parachute.

Option C:
The HE1 Heritage parachute hook by Partridge (see drawing) already has a post on the hook which can be cut to desired length after tying is complete.

Option D:
This could be called by a number of names, Piggyback Nymph by Fran Betters; Parasol Emerger by Ted Leeson and Jim Schollmeyer or a Mary Poppins Nymph by Jack Pangburn. Like all other flies, this one has its good and bad features. At any rate, the idea is to create a ball of deer hair by spinning or cinching a small bundle in the middle with a length of thread or monofilament. The tag end is attached to the top of the hook, ideally under the nymph wing case. If you can imagine a nymph with an umbrella, that is my Mary Poppins. The good point is the buoyant deer hair allows nymph to drift through the water. A bad point is that the tethered line attached to the parachute can on occasion wrap around the hook. This is why fly tying is so much fun.

Chapter 5: *Dubbing*

Isonychia Parachute

Many fly patterns have been developed to imitate the *Isonychia*. Some nymph patterns are of course the Isonychia Nymph, Leadwing Coachman, Zug Bug and the Prince Nymph, to name a few. The nymphs are streamlined like a torpedo and are very fast swimmers. They live in medium to fast currents where they cling to rocks and are capable of swimming in the fast water when necessary. Other slow or non-swimming nymphs are left to the mercy of the currents until they find something on which to cling. *Isonychia* are found in almost all trout waters of the Northeast and emerge pretty much all season. These facts indicate that a few nymph and dry patterns of various sizes would be good additions to your fly box. During the hatch, a few dry-fly patterns are needed so that they can show their stuff on the water's surface; dry-fly patterns include the Adams, Leadwing Coachman Dun, the Slate Drake, a White Gloved Howdy and the Mahogany Dun.

Isonychia Mahogany Dun

(A dry-fly pattern with horizontal hackle around a deer-hair parachute post.)

Hook: Dry Mustad 94840, size 10-14
Thread: Olive
Tail: Elk mane tips
Body: Gray-brown dubbing of muskrat or Antron (SLF)
Wing Post: Natural deer hair
Hackle: Coachman (red-brown)

Dub: to add; transfer of material to something or add to.

Salt Marsh Caterpillar

The salt marsh caterpillar is the larval stage of the Acrea Moth. The larvae are abundant in the fall before over-wintering as pupae in cocoons.

The woolly bear is well known, but the amount of black on each end of its body does not foretell the harshness of the coming winter as predicted in old tales. Both caterpillars are common to the middle of North America, notably the United States.

The Woolly Worm fly is a do-it-all imitation for caterpillars and much more. Many fly fishermen claim the Woolly Worm or Woolly Bugger is the only fly they need.

Woolly Bear

Caterpillar

Hook: Mustad 9672, sizes 4-10
Thread: Black 3/0 (This pattern calls for some tugging if you choose to spin the deer-hair hackles at each end)
Rear Hackle: Short deer hair for spinning or grizzly hackle
Rib: Silver or gold colored wire
Body: Yellow floss or yellow dubbing and chopped deer hair in a thread loop bottle-brush style
Overbody: Peacock herl tied in over back
Front Hackle: Same as rear hackle

Deer Hair Woolly Worm

Hook: Mustad 79580 4x long, sizes 2-14
Thread: Black
Tail: Red yarn or red hackle fibers
Body: Yellow deer hair and SLF dubbing bottle-brush loop (chenille) wrapped on hook shank
Rib: Gold wire for durability followed with grizzly hackle palmered in the same path
Head: Black thread

Borsten

Hook: Long-shank Mustad 9672, sizes 10-18
Thread: Yellow or mustard color
Body: If weighted the hook is wound with copper wire. Construct a bottle-brush loop of black, brown and olive-green deer hair, wind dubbing loop onto hook shank and trim as illustrated.
Head: Yellow thread

Some caddis larvae build houses with plant materials. When this cased worm imitation is weighted it is fished slowly along the bottom. Unweighted the fly becomes an imitation of a floating caterpillar.

Mayflies

Insects are the most successful of all animals in terms of sheer numbers and in their diversity of forms and habitats. There needs to be a lot of insects as they serve as an important food item for many other creatures including bears, foxes, mice, snakes and of course fish.

Insects in the trout's diet may be aquatic, those spending part or all their life in the water, or terrestrial, living on land and falling into the water by some cause. Of the aquatic insects, mayflies, stoneflies, caddisflies and midges are most significant to the fly fisher and consequently the fly tier. Terrestrial insects of note to the fly-fisher include ants, grasshoppers and beetles.

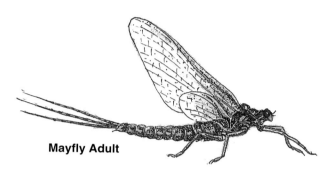

Mayfly Adult

The short-lived, winged mayflies are the cornerstone of modern dry-fly fishing. These insects range in size from 1/8 inch to one and a half inches in length. Their colors cover the natural spectrum of earthy hues; creams, yellows, tans, browns, grays, olives and black. Mayflies normally live for one year, all but a few days of this time is spent in the aquatic stage called a nymph.

Mayfly nymphs are of four basic designs, depending upon their adaptations to the particular stream conditions where they are found.

- Tusked burrowers that live in the silt and fine gravel.
- Flattened clingers that live in fast water.
- Cylindrical-shaped crawlers.
- Torpedo-shaped swimmers.

Regardless of their particular body design, all mayfly nymphs have one visible pair of wing pads and gills on the upper surface of their abdomens.

Burrower Nymph

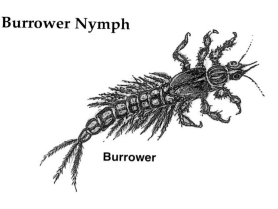

Burrower

The nymphs of the biggest mayflies fall into the burrowing category. A few may reach two inches in length. Burrowers, as the name implies, live in the bottom, out of sight, in tunnels, buried in sand and fine gravel during most of the daylight hours. These large nymphs forage along the bottom at night or during low-light conditions. Use a dark brown Woolly Bugger at dusk, overcast days or at night after dark. Fish the nymph in slow waters that have a soft, firm bottom or sandy gravel. Your choice of nymph color in most cases should be similar to the bottom color. Most common burrower nymphs are brown to ochre (yellow-tan) and in hook sizes from 6 to 10.

Some adult mayfly patterns that descended from the burrower nymphs: Eastern Green Drake, Coffin Fly, sizes 4-6; Yellow Drake, Cream Variant, March Brown, Chocolate Dun and Evening Dun in size 10.

Clinger Nymphs

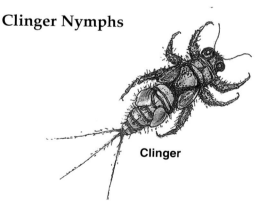

Clinger

A nymph that hugs to the bottom stones and lives behind and between big rocks in fast-water rapids and riffles is a clinger. A beadhead version of the G.R.H.E., Gold Ribbed Hare's Ear nymph or a Fox

Squirrel nymph are recommended imitations tied in sizes 12-18. The imitation needs weight, either a bead head or lead-wire wraps on the hook, to keep the fly on the bottom. A more realistic approach would be to lash pontoons of lead wire to the sides of the hook before adding the body material. The end result will be a flat, broad body that looks like a clinger nymph. The body colors should again mimic the colors of the bottom, varying from tan-olive to brown-black.

Some adult mayfly patterns that descended from the clinger nymphs: March Brown, Ginger Quill, Gray Fox, Light Cahill in size #10; Quill Gordon, Iron Dun, Pale Evening Dun, and the Sulphur in sizes 10-12; the Red Quill and the Olive Dun in size 14.

Crawler Nymphs

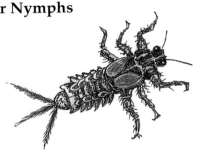

Colors of these crawler nymphs vary with their environment. The bottom background colors range from light brown to red brown (sienna) or dark brown to almost black. Some nymphs living in vegetation will be cream-tan to brown-olive in the size range of the Tricos, size 22 to a large size 8-10 Green Drake. The crawler nymphs average 14-16 hook size.

A rule of thumb for fishing crawler nymphs would be to use a Gold Ribbed Hare's Ear or a Pheasant Tail in the color of the nymph's living habitat. If and when the recommended hook size is listed as 14-16 or 18-20, go with the smaller hook size. If you doubt the logic, tie a smaller nymph onto the larger nymph as a trailer. Keep a record of which nymph accounts for the most fish. Could it be because the small nymph is at the end of the line that it attracts more attention?

Some adult mayfly patterns that descended from the crawler nymphs: Hendrickson, Red Quill, and Lady Beaverkill in sizes 10-12; Pale Evening Dun, Sulphur, Blue-winged Olive, Blue-winged Mahogany, and the Iron Blue Dun are a few in sizes 14-16; the White Wing Black Trico in the tiny sizes of 20-26.

Swimmer Nymphs

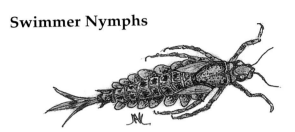

The olive and gray colored swimmer nymphs camoflage nicely. They spend most of the time feeding in the algae and aquatic vegetation. When disturbed, they make use of their swimming speed and escape to the bottom rocks for protection. It is during this movement through the water that trout notice them.

The Pheasant Tail Flashback nymph is the best fly pattern to imitate the long slender body of the swimmer nymph. Tied on an extra-long hook shank in sizes 12-20 with some flash material to reflect light and help attract the trouts' attention. According to the rules of nature, the natural's colors blend in with its habitat. The most noticeable of these colors are olive, brown and gray. You would do well to have a series of Pheasant Tail Flashback nymphs of these colors in sizes 14-20 for each color. The nymph is a swimmer, so when fishing it, make it move with short, jerky and brisk retrieves.

Some of the adult mayfly patterns that descended from swimmer nymphs: Gray and Slate Drakes in sizes 8-10; Leadwing Coachman, Mahogany Dun and Isonychia in sizes 10-12; Blue-winged Olives sizes 16-28.

Bottle-Brush Dubbing Loop

This procedure will render a dubbing item similar in looks to a chenille pipe cleaner.

The dubbing spinner illustrated was made for me by Herman Abrams, a friend, the manufacturer. The precisely balanced brass tool is available in many fly-tying supply shops.

  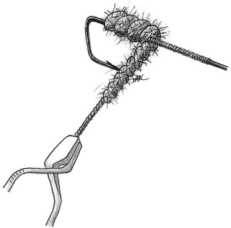

Step 1: Use tacky dubbing wax to coat base thread. Any one of the following materials can be used to change the base thread for purpose of color, size and strength of the chenille: threads of varied colors, Swannundaze, yarn, metalic and fancy threads or string.

Step 2: Refer to A and B in Illustration 1. Lay fur, hair or hackle across the base thread at 90 degrees as shown. Overlay the material with the top thread from point A. Point A being a pin, brad or vise clamped hook. Form the dubbing loop by hooking thread to a spinner hook at Point B.

Step 3: Refer to Illustration 2. The spinning loop twists the thread and traps the material in a spiral-like chenille ready for wrapping on a hook shank as in Illustration 3. Attach a hackle clamp or similar tool to keep chenille from unwinding; the clamp also serves as a handle.

Deer Hair Nymph
The Gold Ribbed Hare's Ear

No one knows for certain who originally designed this fly but James Ogden, a tyer during Victorian times, is on the top of the list. During the late 1800s the pattern was fished as a dry fly.

The fly's shaggy appearance resembles many species of nymphs. A proper-sized pattern mimics a mayfly nymph quite well. Teasing or picking-out hair fibers from the thorax dubbing makes a good representation of legs and helps to make the fly appear alive as it moves in the water. The most common method of fishing this deer-hair nymph is to float a greased, unweighted fly on a dead drift to imitate a surface-hatching mayfly. A weighted nymph short-lined as an aquatic insect along the bottom, around rocks and vegetation, has proved to be very successful for me. Move the fly slowly and smoothly in a crawling mode. Every once in awhile, jerk the line to dart the fly forward as though it were escaping. Movement such as this will usually induce a strike by an observing trout.

Deer Hair Nymph

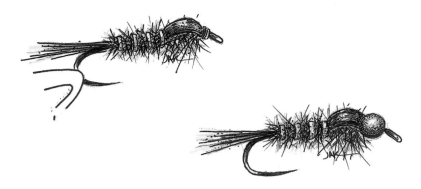

Hook: Nymph 2X long Mustad 3906B, size 8-16
Thread: Gray
Tail: Deer hock hair or brown quill fibers
Underbody: Lead-free wire weight (optional)
Rib: Gold wire or gold tinsel
Abdomen: Natural deer body hair dubbing
    (bottle-brush chenille)
Wingcase: Mottled brown/black turkey wing quill section
Thorax: Natural dark deer-hair dubbing with legs picked out
    from the sides

Step 1: Attach thread at hook bend above barb, mount tail hairs on top of hook shank and bind down with tips extended a hook-gap length.

Step 2: Optional weight: beginning at butt end of tail, start wrapping lead-free wire on the hook shank with tight, touching coils. Eight to twelve wraps is usually about right. Use wire of the same size diameter as the hook, leave tie-off space behind the hook eye. A brass beadhead could be used, instead of the wire, by slipping the bead over the hook point and push it up snug to the hook eye.

Step 3: Cocoon the lead-free wire coils with thread wraps. Build a thread taper in front of the last wire coil and return wrap thread to rear of hook to just above the barb. (If a bead head is used, build a thread dam behind the bead to hold it in place. Return thread as above.)

Step 4: At this position tie-in a length of gold wire or tinsel.

Step 5: With the thread at the same position, add the cut-up deer hair to the thread by using dubbing wax and the two strands of thread to spin a bottle-brush dubbing loop.

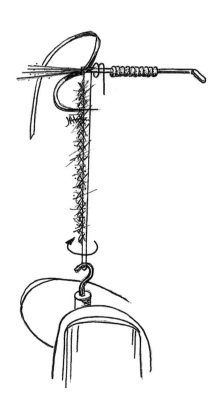

Step 6: Wrap the dubbed thread chenille forward covering 2/3 of the hook creating the abdomen of the nymph.

Step 7: At this 2/3 junction, tie-down one end of the turkey wing quill slip on top of the hook with the best-marked side facing down, dull side up.

Step 8: Spiral wrap the ribbing, wire or tinsel, over the dubbed abdomen from the rear with 4 or 5 evenly spaced wraps and tie off in front of the wing slip.

Step 9: In front of the wing quill slip, start dubbing the thorax area. Keep in mind you are trying to achieve a shaggy body. After the fly is finished, some of these fibers will be picked or teased out to serve as legs for the nymph.

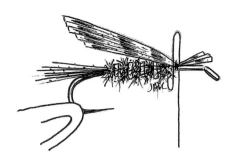

Step 10: Pull the feather strip down over the thorax forming a nymph wing case and secure behind the hook eye with a few tight wraps. Trim the excess feather strip and finish the head. Some tiers like to put a couple coats of tying cement on the wing case for a bit of shine and durability. Pick out some fibers from the thorax to represent legs with a dubbing needle. Remember, shaggy is better.

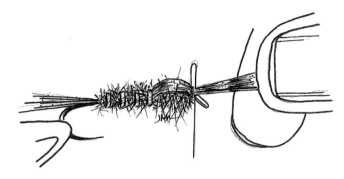

DST Compara Dun
(Allan Podell, Elmira, NY)

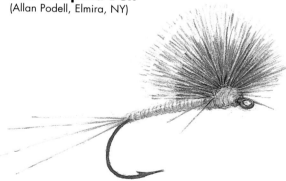

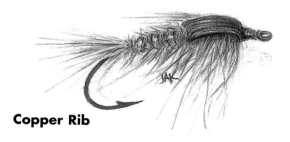

Copper Rib

Flashback

Hook: Mustad 94840 Dry, size 12-16
Thread: Yellow
Wing: Hollow gray deer hair upright and flared
Tail: Olive Micro Fibetts
Body: Yellow DST quills

Allan Podell, an accomplished fly tier and member of the Catskill Fly Tying Guild, tied the deer-hair fly patterns in my illustration.

Scuds

Scuds are small, 3/16 to three quarters of an inch long, shrimp-looking crustaceans, often called freshwater shrimp. Scuds are found almost exclusively in alkaline  waters and trout actively seek out these nutrient-rich bits of energy. When abundant in numbers they contribute to the enrichment and growth rate of the trout that feed on them. To off-set such predacious activity the scuds are very prolific. When carrying eggs the female scud takes on an orange color. This can happen six or more times a year, so it is important to always carry a few orange scuds in your fly box. Another good reason is that many scuds often die off in large numbers, turning orange-brown as they die.

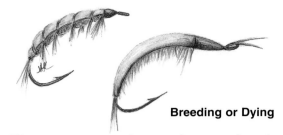

Breeding or Dying

The gray-green scuds are only seen when they are swimming after being dislodged from vegetation. An important element in tying a swimming scud is to use a straight-shank hook because when the scud swims its body is completely straight. The scud bends into its characteristic curled position only when it crawls and scuttles about the vegetation, or is dead, but then it is orange not green.

Swimming

Orange Deer Hair Scud

Hook: Curved Mustad 80050, size12-22
Thread: Orange
Tail and Body: Orange dyed deer hair or bucktail
Body Appendages: Chopped orange deer hair dubbed on mid
   section of hook
Shellback: Clear or frosted narrow plastic bag strips or Flashabou

Step 1: Tie some loose deer hair length-wise on top of the hook shank, wind the thread palmer fashion to the eye of the hook. Lightly dub the thread with chopped deer hair and dubbing wax and wind to the rear of the hook.

Step 2: With the thread at the rear of the hook, tie-in a thin strip of plastic or 2-3 thin strips of Flashabou. Pull plastic forward, representing a scud back, and palmer thread over the plastic, around the body dubbing back to the hook eye and finish head.

Step 3: Pick out some body fibers to mimic the multileg appendages.

Iridescent Dubbing

The flies I have illustrated are from Ronn Lucas, Sr. Ronn sent me these flies tied with his iridescent dubbing, it's available from many tying supply catalogs as well as from him.

Ronn Lucas, Sr.
13535 SE Beech
Milwaukie, OR 97267

The iridescent dubbing can be used solo or mixed with deer hair and furs. The flashback material he offers comes in different colors and is very effective used as shell-backs on beetles, scuds and flashback nymphs.

Check www.flyanglersonline.com to view some of Ronn's excellent fantasy salmon-fly creations.

Debris Caddis (Detritus)

08 Cream iridescent dubbing mixed with chopped deer hair, 44 Green Peacock and 10 Burgundy added to fly head.
The numbers indicate the color reference code.

Adult Damsel

26 Sapphire blue iridescent mix body dubbing with natural deer hair tail and wings.

Grease Liner

10 Burgundy and 05 Brown body dubbing with dark deer-hair tail, wing and head. Tier, Harry Leviere.

Cajun Caddis

16 Orange iridescent body palmered with gold tinsel, ginger hackle with natural deer-hair wing.

The deer (elk) caddis is the only dry fly you need. It offers everything—super floatation, great visibility and good durability. It's a killer during the caddis hatch, but produces quite well fished as a searching pattern. Usually the fly is fished dead-drift, but because of the full hackle rib, it also allows the fisherman to skate the fly across the water's surface. The bushy buoyant deer-hair dubbing also keeps the fly riding high, like a cork, in fast, bumpy water. For flat water, you can trim the hackle flush with the bottom of the fly, this puts the fly right on the surface or in the foam. Move the fly in a fluttering motion to simulate preflight or egg depositing.

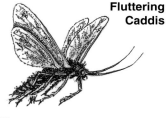

Fluttering Caddis

Deer Hair Caddis

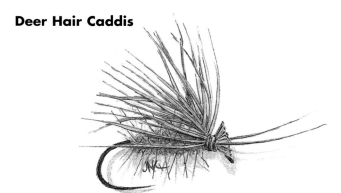

Hook: Dry, Mustad 94840, size 12-18
Thread: Gray
Tail: None
Body: SLF (synthetic living fiber) dubbing blended with deer hair. Suggested colors are tan, brown, olive or gray and sometimes black on the smaller sized hooks
Hackle: Color of choice, usually in contrast to the body color
Wing: Natural deer hair tied in at the head just behind the hook eye, trim excess at same angle as hook eye
Notes: Infuse twisted dubbing loop with chopped deer hair to represent legs instead of using palmered hackle. Use short hair from the deer hocks or mask in the dubbing mix. Antennae are optional, if added use two stripped hackle stems.

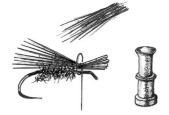

Step 1: Wind thread from tie-in point behind the eye to the hook bend. Dub the chopped deer hair and body material to a waxed section of thread. Form the dubbing loop and twist body material mixed with chopped deer hair as hackle between the two strands of thread to make a "spikey noodle".

Step 2: The noodle with the chopped hair mixed in represents legs and body all in one application. Wind on hook, stopping behind the eye and leaving enough room to tie in the deer-hair bundle to be used in forming the wing and head.

Step 3: Use hair stacker to even off the tip ends facing the tail. Distribute the hair to portray fluttering wings.

Step 4: Trim the butt ends of deer-hair wing bundle to form the head.

Note: If antennae are desired, tie stripped hackle stems, fox whiskers or paintbrush bristles to the hook at the head anchor point.

The Compara-dun was developed in the Catskills by Al Caucci during the 1960s. The features are very similar to the older Haystack pattern by Fran Betters of the Adirondack area.

Mayfly

The Compara-dun is one of the most universally effective fly designs for matching mayfly hatches. The body of the fly rides flush against the water because there is no hackle. This presents a well-defined profile of the body. The wing keeps the fly upright and makes a great flatwater pattern. If deer hair was used in rendering the body it adds buoyancy which allows the fly to hang-on even in rough water.

Compara-Dun Mayfly

Hook: Dry, Mustad 94840 Size #10-20
Thread: Gray or brown
Tail: Dark strands of bucktail or body hair
Body: Blended dubbing (color to match natural mayfly) Finely chopped deer hair mixed in aids in the floatation.
Wing: Deer body hair tied in an arc of 180 degrees on top of the hook extending from one side of the body to the other side like a fan

Step 1: Even the tip ends of a small bunch of fine deer hair, bind down to hook with butts facing tail at the one-third point behind the eye.

Step 2: Push the tip ends of the hair-wing upright and place a few wraps of thread at the base and in front of the wing to keep it upright. Distribute the hair fibers to create a fan wing of 180 degrees from one side to the other.

Step 3: Wind thread back over wing butts to the bend of the hook and attach tail fibers. At the tail-body junction, form a dubbing loop and twist the dubbing to produce a "noodle".

Step 4: Wrap noodle on hook shank to form fly body, remove excess noodle material from the thread and make a small thread head in front of the wings.

Chapter 7: *Wulff Patterns*

The Wulff patterns were the first flies to use hair for wings and tails. The Gray Wulff was the earliest known Wulff hairwing pattern of the now-famous series by Lee Wulff, the man who first promoted "catch and release" fishing. He claimed that a nice fish was too valuable to be caught only once.

Variants of the same style of pattern include the Adams Wulff, the White Wulff, the Ausable Wulff and many others. All are good floaters on rippled water and are large enough to be seen by both fish and fishermen with diminishing eyesight.

Gray Wulff

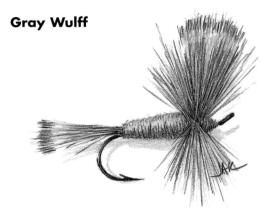

Hook: Dry, Mustad 94840 or Mustad 36890 salmon hook, Sizes 8-16
Thread: Gray
Wing: Natural deer body hair
Tail: Natural deer body hair
Body: Gray dubbing (muskrat color)
Hackle: Medium gray-blue dun
Note: This pattern is large enough to mimic the March brown, the green and brown drakes and other large mayflies.

March Brown

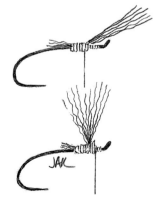

Step 1: Tie a bunch of deer hair on top of the hook a short space behind the hook eye. Lift the front portion up-right, and divide in half with a figure-eight wrapping.

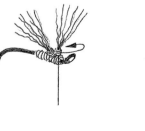

Step 2: Wind the thread to the hook bend covering the butt ends of the wing hair. Tie a few pieces of deer hair at the bend for the tail. Wax the thread and dub with gray wool, fur or Antron and wrap the fly body to behind the wing with a smooth taper.

Step 3: Attach and wind on a medium gray hackle behind and in front of the wing base. Finish fly with a small thread head.

Flared Bucktail Bodies

The flared bucktail in this case does not imitate wings but bodies made of bucktail hair. When two hooks are tied in tandem it allows for a fly of extra length, two "breathing" sections with a bend-in-the-middle "wiggle" afforded by a flexible connection.

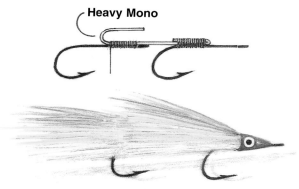

Flared Bucktail In Tandem

When it comes to tying and fishing large flies, consider this situation: you have two pieces of pie on a plate, one small and one larger piece, which one would you take? In a similar underwater scene: two flies, one large, one small; do you think a hungry fish would take the smaller fly? I posed a similar question elsewhere in another section.

Making large, colorful big-fish flies requires a few decisions. You have the option of buying pre-dyed deer hair and bucktails or purchasing the natural colored hair and bleaching and dying for yourself. The cost factor for each option must be considered. The data presented here is an estimated average of costs for each option:

- Dyed saltwater bucktails, hair length of 4 inches plus, choice of 12 colors, $5.45 each.
- Bucktails small to medium, white only $2.75 each
- Dyed large bucktails, 18 colors, $4.00 each
- Jumbo bucktails, white only $4.25 each
- Dyed white deer belly hair for spinning, 2x3-inch patch, 14 colors $2.50 each
- Acid dyes for feathers and hair, 14 colors, one ounce single color $8.25
- Concentrated dye (half teaspoon per quart of water) 18 colors half ounce $5.95

Check out the fly tying and angler supply houses before making your decision.

Atlantic Silverside

Silverside, Spearing, Shiner

Silversides are migratory baitfish found swimming near the surface in and around inlets, bays and beaches. Their schools are composed of fish nearly the same size. They get blitzed from dusk to dawn by such predators as striped bass, bluefish, bonito, weakfish and flounder. Sometimes called spearing or shiner minnows, these fish range in size from two to five inches long. Tandem streamers or bendbacks provide for a longer fly to imitate this baitfish. Tan, white, olive, gray and pale green bucktail in the right proportions, the placement of prominent eyes and some red paint added to the throat or gill area will give you a nice minnow pattern for both salt- and fresh-water fishing.

Chesapeake Bucktail

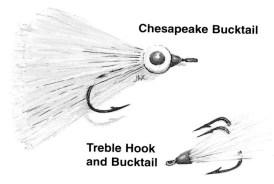

Chesapeake Bucktail

Treble Hook and Bucktail

This is a striped bass fly with a body of dyed deer hair tied on just behind the hook eye. The tier has a choice of many colors and color combinations. The hair should be flared evenly around the hook. The fly is finished after gluing on a pair of over-sized eyes.

The Chesapeake Bucktail is often tied on a strong treble hook for more hook-up ability. Fish the fly with a jerk-and-pull method that causes the deer hair to open and collapse with enticing movement. This fly is often tied with marabou feathers alone or in combination with the deer hair to enhance this movement.

Tarpon Streamers

Green Machine

Tail: Four to six dyed yellow-green saddle hackles tied on at the top of the hook bend. Feathers should curve outward to each side

Collar: Dyed deer hair optional color spun and flared evenly

Neckband: Tying thread used to bind down butt ends of deer-hair collar

Nose: Continue tapering the thread down to the hook eye. Epoxy and coat with paint and varnish

Eyes: Plastic oversize eyes of contrasting color glued on with epoxy

Black and White Cockroach

Tail: Natural grizzly saddle hackle

Collar: Brown deer hair, flared

Band: Black thread, epoxy and paint

Neck: No taper, show bare hook with option to taper thread as illustrated

Pacific Coast Candlefish

Long Trailing Bucktail

Chapter 9: *Spinning*

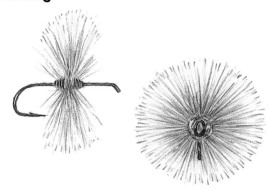

Spinning Deer Hair

The Skitterbug fly is an easy one to learn how and where to use the spinning technique. The finished fly can be successfully used as a spider, a daddy longlegs, crane fly or a skittering caddis laying her eggs. A controlled line and a little breeze or current will make this fly literally skate on its edges.

Skitterbug

Hook: Dry, Mustad 94840, size 10-14
Thread: Gray
Hackle: Natural deer body hair
Note: Spin a bunch of deer hair with butt ends facing back towards hook bend. Spin another bunch of the same size with the butt ends facing front toward hook eye. Trim-cut the butts of both front and back bunches as close to hook shank as possible. Anchor both ends with thread wraps and cement.

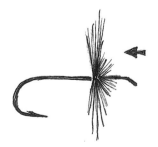

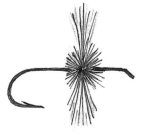

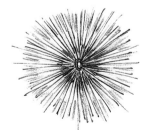

Step 1: Cut off a small bunch of natural deer body hair from the hide patch. Hold the bunch of hair on top of the hook and take three loose turns of thread over the top. Pull down on the

thread, as it tightens the hair will flare out and spin around the hook.

Step 3: Repeat steps as necessary and trim.

Front view.

Dahlberg Diver

The Dahlberg Diver was designed by Larry Dahlberg to be fished deep with its high collar giving off water vibrations and the long tails to attracting attention.

Because the fly fishes deep near fly-grabbing stuff like weeds, debris and the bottom you may want to tie in a weed guard (see note before Step 7).

Dahlberg Diver

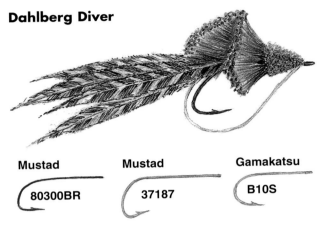

Hook: Mustad 80300BR or 37187 also Gamakatsu B10S round bend, large size 2-10
Thread: White or red 3/0
Weed Guard: Heavy monofilament
Wings: Brown or grizzly saddle hackles (Option, use a strip of rabbit fur to replace the hackles)
Collar: Deer hair dyed red
Head: Deer hair dyed red; spun and clipped to shape

Step 1: Tie in two pair of hackles at the bend on each side of the hook; feathers should flare out to each side.

Step 2: Tie in a bunch of deer- hair on top of the hook just in front of the hackle butts. The deer hair butts should face forward.

Step 3: Loop the bunch of deer hair with several soft loops to secure. Do not allow the tips to flare. Hold the bunch of deer hair to keep it from spinning. The tips facing the rear will be the outside edge of the collar.

Step 4: Tie in and spin several bunches of deer hair directly in front of the last; continue this adding, flaring, spinning and packing the deer hair until the hook shank is covered. Save space behind the eye to whip-finish. Rotate the hook to be upside-down and trim the bottom flat and as close to the shank as possible.

Step 5: Return hook to right side-up and trim the front half of the spun deer hair to a bullet shape. Leave the collar of deer hair at the back of the head. Trim the collar to a rounded flare about twice the body diameter.

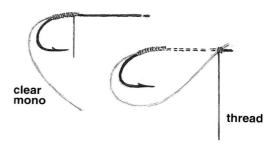

clear
mono

thread

Note: If a weed guard is employed, start the fly by attaching a length of heavy mono to the hook bend. (See illustration) Reattach thread to hook-eye and push loose end of mono through eye forming a smooth curve a bit larger than the hook gape. Fold mono back over head and fasten with thread, whip-finish and cement.

Adult Dragonfly and Damselfly

An adult dragonfly or damselfly is not a good food source for trout or bass because most of the time they are out of reach, being above the water surface. The nymph, on the other hand, is readily available and makes a sizable morsel of food.

Most dragonflies and damselflies are identified only in the adult stage; sometimes called mosquito hawks or darning needles. Nymphs of both species are much alike in appearance; both are dull-colored, awkward-looking creatures. Adult dragonflies hold their wings in a horizontal position when resting, the smaller, delicate damselflies hold their

Adult Dragonfly

Adult Damselfly

wings upward and backward. (Note the illustration)

Strawman

The Strawman is a spun deer-hair-bodied fly that floats. This fly and the Floating Dragonfly Nymph though not often used for nymph patterns; spun deer hair, or any hollow hair from antelope or caribou, can be used to form bulky, light bodies. When fishing these flies, weight is added up the leader from the fly to sink it. The buoyancy of these bodies will cause the fly to float above the weight. This allows a fly to be fished above submerged rocks or weeds without snagging.

Strawman

Hook: Nymph, 2X, 3X long, sizes 8-14
Thread: Dark brown
Tail: Short deer hair (hock or mask)
Body: Deer hair spun
Hackle: Gray, teal or grizzly
Head: Dark brown thread

Bear Dragon

Hook: Streamer, sizes 8-14
Thread: Brown
Tail and Body: (note illustration) Deer hair is spun on the hook in two sections with the front section overlapping the rear section
Head: Tapered thread head

Floating Dragonfly Nymph

Hook: Nymph, 3X, 4X long, sizes 4-10
Thread: Olive or brown
Tail: Brown deer hair
Body: Olive or brown deer hair spun (note illustration)
Legs: Olive or brown deer hair
Wing Case: Turkey wing feather section, cut to shape and coated with cement
Eyes: Black plastic
Head: Olive brown dubbing

Adult Caddis

Mayflies were the insect group that originally provided the natural models for tying fishing flies; caddisfly imitations were not far behind. Caddis have long since gained popularity because they are the predominant insect in many of the world's trout waters.

Resting Sedge/Caddis

The caddisfly undergoes a complete metamorphosis by progressing through a life cycle of several various stages. During the adult cycle the wings of the insect, when still, form a tent over the back, long antennae extend from the heads of their gray and brown colored bodies.

Goddard Caddis

The best way to fish an adult caddis is to skitter and skip the fly across the water surface, imitating preflight or egg depositing.

The John Goddard Caddis makes a pretty good impostor for a resting adult caddis. The pattern requires spinning, packing and trimming deer hair similar to the procedures for the Muddler and Strawman. Hackle is employed for legs; however a few strands of deer hair left untrimmed on each side will serve as a substitute for hackle legs.

The fly can imitate a wide number of large caddis or sedge (English). The wing design is unique because of its construction and trimming. (Note the illustrations show two different ways to handle the wings.

Goddard Caddis or Sedge

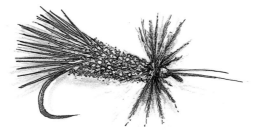

Hook: Up-eyed Mustad salmon 3689 or long-shank 79580
Thread: Gray or brown
Hackle: Red-brown, ginger or furnace
Antennae: Hackle with barbs removed

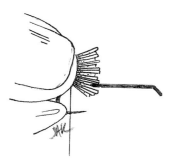

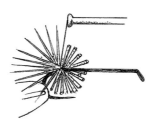

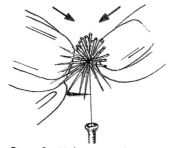

Step 1: Attach a bunch of cut deer hair on the hook shank by following the illustrated steps. Wind the tying thread loosely around the hook shank and the deer hair twice.

Step 2: Complete the second turn by pulling down on the thread, and at the same time releasing your finger hold on the deer hair. The hair will spin around the hook shank and flare out.

Step 3: Make a couple extra turns with the thread, push the flared hair from the back and the front using the Brassie tool or by using your thumb and fingernails to compact the spun deer hair. Add a touch of cement to the thread.

Step 4: Repeat Steps 1, 2, and 3 until the hook shank is full, except for the hackle area just behind the hook eye.

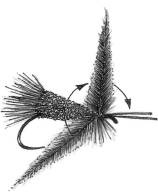

Step 5: Cut and trim the compacted deer hair to form the Goddard Caddis body and wing profile. Leave the tail end untrimmed. Select two hackles, a brown and ginger. Strip the fibers from the butt end of the stem to a length desired for the antennae and tie them on. Leaving the stems forward as antennae, wrap the remaining hackle stem of each hackle around the hook shank behind the eye. Finish with a small thread head.

Goddard Caddis (Variant)

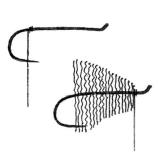

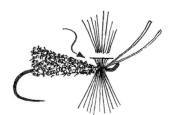

Step 1: Spin deer hair onto hook shank (*Note illustrations*).

Step 2: Clip the deer hair to shape as shown, a somewhat flat bottom (Note: *The original Goddard Caddis had the tail section of spun deer hair left long. The Goddard variant's tail has been neatly trimmed.*)

Step 3: The hackles are wound on in the normal manner; on the original, the hackles are left untrimmed. The variant's hackle has been trimmed across the top, leaving the bottom hackle as a beard.

Step 4: The stripped hackle stems are tied in place as antennae. Finish with small thread head.

Deer Hair Mouse

A deer-hair fly pattern to try when you have a lot of time.

Muddler Minnow

The cockatush minnow is a small bullhead-like goby found in North America. The Wisconsin nickname for this little fish is "muddler". Other names for the small minnow are "sculpin" or "bullhead".

During the late 1940s, Don Gapen, of the Gapen Fly Company in Minnesota, created the Muddler to imitate the mottled sculpin minnow. (Sculpin are a small, spiny, bottom-loving fish with a broad head and a wide mouth.) The Muddler fly has become one of the best-known fly patterns. No other fly can come close to it for versatility. Depending on how it is finished and fished, it can represent a terrestrial insect, a minnow or even a large nymph. The original Muddler brought about a large number of variations, all of which have the spun and clipped deer-hair head; such as the Goddard Caddis and the Strawman. The buoyant deer hair allows the Muddler to be fished at all depths. Fished deep near the bottom it resembles a sculpin; fished still and floating on the surface it portrays a terrestrial hopper or show a wake by skating the fly on the surface late in the season and it imitates a fluttering caddis.

Muddler Minnow

Note how the Muddler Minnow is tied, step-by-step; the tail section, the body, under wing and paired turkey wing quill slips are laid over the back. The head and collar made of deer hair is spun on the hook just behind the hook eye, folded backwards and trimmed. A tip: after you have finished spinning the deer hair on the hook, take a piece of plastic drinking straw about 3/4" long, slice the piece lengthwise. Slip the straw over the head of the fly, covering the deer hair needed for the collar. None of the collar hair will be cut off while trimming the head to shape. A razor blade, scissors or an electric beard trimmer have all been used to shape the fly head, use what works for you. Some tiers have been known to scorch the spun deer hair head after trimming. Of course this darkens the head, and claims have been made that the flame seals the cut ends to make them waterproof.

Muddler Minnow

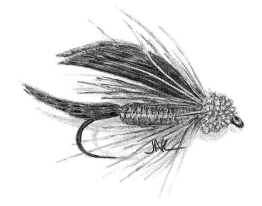

Hook: Streamer Mustad 79580 or 9575, sizes 2-8
        Hopper (Surface fly) Mustad 9671 or 9672, sizes 8-12;
        Caddis (Surface fly) Mustad 9484, sizes 10-14
Thread: Gray 6/0 for tying 3/0 for spinning
Tail: Pair mottled turkey wing quill slips
Body: Flat gold tinsel (Options)
Wing: Long white bucktail hair as under-wing support, over which
        are another pair of mottled turkey wing quill sections
Head and Collar: Natural deer hair spun and clipped as shown

Preparing Wing-Quill Slip

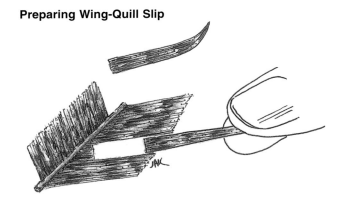

Preparing Deer-Hair Patch

Brassie

Step 1: Wrap the tying thread to the bend of the hook and tie-in the wing quill slips for the tail, then tie-in a length of flat or oval gold tinsel for wrapping the body. Option: twisted, gold-cord tinsel for wrapping the body produces more bulk in the abdomen. Wind the gold material for the body over the hook shank to near the hook eye. Tie-in a small bunch of white bucktail hair on top of the hook at the head area.

Step 2: On top of the bucktail hair, tie-in the pair of turkey wing quill slips, for the fly wings, one on either side of the hook in a tent fashion covering the white bucktail. Some people tie the wings in with the points up and others with the points down, your choice.

Step 3: The formation of the head; cut off a small bunch of natural deer hair from the patch, clean out the under fluff and short hair and hold the bunch on the hook and take three turns of thread.

Step 4: Pull down on the loose turns of thread and the hair will flare out as the thread tightens. Pack the flared bunch tight with your finger and thumbnails or use a Brassie hair packer; apply a drop of cement and a wrap or two of thread to anchor the hair in place.

Step 5: Repeat Steps 3 and 4 several times until head area is packed full and tight.

Step 6: Using sharp scissors, trim the deer hair to shape, leaving a collar of unclipped hair. Tie off thread just behind the eye.

The finished fly.

Chapter 10: *Bundled Bodies*

Extended-Body Mayflies

Look at a real mayfly and study its basic characteristics or peruse a flyfishing book that discusses the natural fly and its tied imitations. The naturals set low on the water surface and float like small sailboats with wings like sails. They have thin curved extended bodies tapering to a full thorax.

The following illustrations and information will give you direction on how to tie or make a facsimile. You will finish with a realistic-looking fly that has the characteristics of the natural. The list of extended-body flies includes suggested hook size for each particular mayfly. Materials used in tying will vary but the tying procedures and sequences remain the same. If you can tie one you can certainly tie them all.

The giant mayfly size 8 2XL, green and brown drakes size 10 2XL, Eastern yellow drake, March brown and gray fox all on size 12 2XL or size 12 XL. The white mayfly, light Cahill and Hendrickson match up with size 14 hooks.

Step 1: To achieve the elongated body or abdomen for these flies, begin by tying the bucktail hair strands on to a needle or hat pin that has been clamped in the tying vise. Palmer the thread the length of the needle with equal spacing. Return palmer the thread X-crossing the first wrapping. Extend 2 to 3 strands of bucktail beyond the abdomen to serve as a tail. Tie off thread at butt end of the abdomen. The bucktail can be substituted for cock pheasant-tail barbs, peccary bristles, paintbrush bristles, moose or elk mane, and Micro Fibetts.

To complete Step 1, slide the body off the needle or pin, adjust and set the body curve, coat with cement and let dry.

Step 2: The second step is the attachment of the just-completed body to the hook shank. First cocoon the shank with thread and coat with cement before tying on the extended body. This will keep body from rolling and traveling around the hook shank. Tie the body on to the hook at about mid shank. Trim the front of the body of excess length.

Step 3: Options exist for the wings or sails for your fly, including a deer-hair parachute wing. Feathers suitable for wing construction can be found on any up-land game bird or water duck. Some suggested birds are again the cock ringnecked pheasant, hen pheasant, grouse, woodcock, mallard and the teal. Remember they must be a matching pair, one from the left side and one from the right side of the bird. Always buy a full skin so you will have options with regard to pattern, color, size and suitability.

The wing preparation starts with matching a pair of feathers. Next pull off the unwanted fluff and barbs, then hold the pair together with a piece of masking tape on the stems (shaft), or use a drop of hot glue. The wing feathers can be mounted with the curves facing each other, or opposite each other. Using sharp scissors will allow you to cut two feathers to the desired shape at the same time.

A brass clamp wing-burner pattern tool will yield the same size and shape with each use. Two matching feathers are clamped together in the tweezer-like tool and held near a flame. The excess feather unprotected and sticking out around the pattern tool will be burned off, leaving two identical wings.

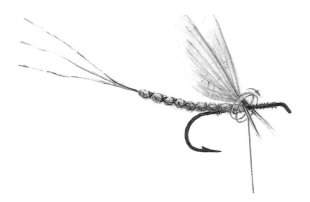

Step 4: Once you're satisfied with the pair of feather wings they need to be attached to the hook. With thread and a touch of cement, tie-in the wings just ahead of the attached body.

Step 5: Vertical hackle is not suitable for the thorax because it causes the fly to ride too high on the water surface. The bottom hackle could be trimmed but then why use vertical hackle? Hackle applied parachute style proves to be satisfactory. The thorax is constructed by wrapping the area with a deer-hair dubbed thread twisted into a chenille rope. Once the thorax is wrapped, use a bodkin or needle to pick-out some of the twisted deer-hair fibers to mimic legs.

The finished fly is ready to sail, the hook serves as a keel and the slightest breeze will power the winged vessel at a delicate pace.

Brown Drake

Nymphs of the brown drake are of the burrower type, they emerge from the sand-gravel mixture in gentle riffles. The hatch occurs mid-June to mid-July after dark. Adults have a tan body, blotched brown wings and three tails. The brown drake hook size of 10 2XL is a larger variation of the March Brown and Gray Fox flies that have two tails.

Cranefly

Cranefly adults look like giant mosquitoes. Where abundant, the craneflies dance around the overhanging grasses at stream edge. A large bushy fly like the Skater cast down stream and twitched slightly on the retrieve will fool fish. Another sample pattern is the extended-body parachute hackle fly with hackle-tip wings.

Cranefly larvae are often called water worms, they range in length from half-inch to three inches. They sometimes are of numbers enough to be a regular item on the menu of trout. The Cranefly Larva Worm is another fly easily constructed by the deer-hair bundling procedure described earlier; add a palmered hackle and trim it short.

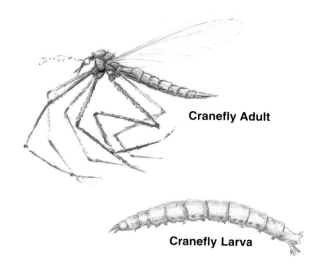

Cranefly Adult

Cranefly Larva

Cranefly Parachute

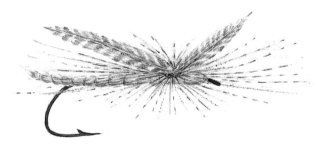

Hook: Mustad 9575 Limerick bend, size 10-12
Thread: Brown
Body: Natural deer hair bundled, try some orange dyed deer hair
Rib: Thread
Wings: Grizzly hackle tips
Hackle: Light gray or tan horizontal, wrap parachute style

Cranefly Larva

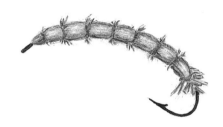

Hook: Mustad 80500BR long curve shank, size 14-6
Thread: Brown
Underbody: Optional weight
Body: Light natural deer hair bundled
Rib: Brown hackle trimmed short

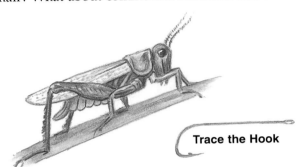

Hopper Variants

Design your own hopper, begin by tracing the hook illustrated or one of your choice. Consider these factors in your pattern design; you need a fly with good floatability and a convincing profile. Are you going to use dubbed, wrapped, bundled or spun buoyant deer hair? What about commercial materials like closed-

Trace the Hook

cell foam; does it have advantages over dyed deer hair? Think through what you are trying to accomplish with your fly pattern and then devise a way to make it perform like you envision. The performance

is going to be dictated by all sorts of factors, weight is one, type of material is another and size are only a few. Remember if weight is added on the leader, above the fly, it allows the buoyant deer-hair pattern to float just above the weight. A good place for a minnow mimic.

To tie the pattern illustrated here, a simple floating fly, put it together by following the same steps as for the other bundled, buoyant deer-hair bodies. At the head, leave some of the folded body deer hair free as a beard resembling legs. Tie-in a pair of wings at the collar to complete the pattern. A painted eye on each side of the head would be an enhancement but not a necessity.

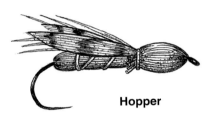

Hopper

D.H. Hopper

Hook: Extra-long Mustad 79580, sizes 6-14 (You might try the new Gamakatsu Stinger B10S)
Thread: Olive yellow or tan
Body: Bundled natural bucktail
Underwing: Natural deer hair
Overwing: Hen pheasant or similar upland game bird mottled feather
Head and Collar: Natural bucktail
Legs: Fluorescent yellow rubber (Clearwater material) or regular rubber band
Note: Clearwater is a soft stretchable polymer strand material available in different colors from: Russ Krahnert
Glenwood Sales Co.
908 N. Glenwood Trail
Southern Pines, NC 28387

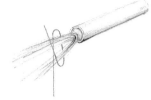

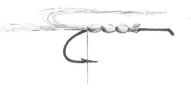

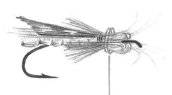

Step 1: Bucktail hair extended past the bend, rib the bundle with thread and then fold the extended deer hair forward over the top. Wrap the folded bundle again with thread.

Step 2: Apply deer hair as underwing for the hen feather or similar, coat with vinyl cement, dry, fold to tent shape and tie-in.

Step 4: Bucktail hair tied in with tips facing forward, then folded backward and tied down with neck band of thread. Attach rubber-band hackle under neck band.

Note: A plastic tube such as a pen cap, expended Flair pen casing or any small tube will work when folding bucktail hair. When you fish the D.H. Hopper you will see how well the fly floats on the surface.

Super Hopper

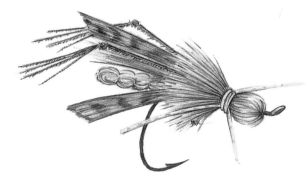

This pattern is tied in a fashion similar to the D.H. Hopper, except for the pheasant-tail barb rear legs and separate wing slips from a mottled feather.

Deer-Hair Beetle

Darkling beetle larvae are the "mealworms" used for feeding birds, small caged pets and fish. The fact that there are a great number of beetles and beetle species, it's a good bet that more than a few of them will fall or be blown onto the water.

Beetle

Beetle

Hook: Dry fly Mustad 94840, size 10-16
Thread: Black
Shellback: Black deer hair
Body: Peacock herl

Step 1: Start thread at mid hook bend.

Step 2: Cut a small bundle of deer hair about the diameter of a pencil. Hold deer hair by tips and comb out short hair and underfur with dubbing needle. Tie-in butt ends of deer hair to the mid point on the hook bend. Butts will flare when thread pulls tight. Bind butts to hook with butts facing hook eye. Tie-in the tips of several strands of peacock herl just ahead of deer-hair tie-in point. Wind thread forward to behind hook eye.

Step 3: Wrap the strands of herl around the hook to the eye, fasten with a few turns of thread. Fold the deer hair forward over the herl and tie down behind the eye, forming a shellback. Make several wraps with thread, and half-hitch to finish.

Step 4: Trim excess hair tips and herl at same angle as hook eye. Clip a couple deer-hair strands from each side at rear of body, fold forward as legs. Apply several coats of cement or varnish to produce a hard shellback if desired.

Black Ant

Carpenter ants make up one of the largest groups of ants. They live in dead wood, logs and building timbers. Carpenter ants are found in all temperate regions of the world. It is safe to say that a black ant pattern would not be unknown to any fish in these regions.

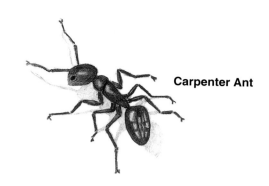

Carpenter Ant

Winged Black Ant

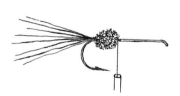

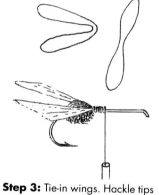

Step 1: Tie a small clump of black deer hair onto bend of hook. Trim the butt ends. Add some black dubbing over the tie-in point to form a ball.

Step 2: Pull deer hair over the ball to form the back of the abdomen. Trim the excess ends of deer hair.

Step 3: Tie-in wings. Hackle tips make good-looking delta wings when tied in flat. They of course can be tied-in at a slant. (Note: To make your own wing shapes, cut them from either a clear or white plastic bag. The length of each wing usually equals the length of the body. There is also commercial wing material available.)

Step 4: The addition of hackle in the middle of the hook creates the illusion of legs and adding another ball of dubbing for the head completes the fly.

Crayfish

Crayfish, sometimes called crabs or craw-dads, live and thrive in all types of water; slow or fast moving, cold or warm, clear or discolored. Most crayfish spend their time hiding on the bottom under rocks or debris. They are primarily nocturnal, saving their activity until after dark. Crayfish move in two ways, on the bottom they normally crawl forward slowly. When threatened, they crawl backward with their pincers raised. Other than those pincers, their best defense is to

Crayfish

swim in a fast, darting, backward motion for protection. Fly-fishermen casting a crayfish pattern would do best fishing after dark and by either moving the fly across the bottom slowly or jerking the fly in a short, fast motion. Be ready for a strike when you fish the crawfish in this way, a following fish usually goes into attack mode.

Crayfish

Hook: Mustad 79580, sizes 4-8 streamer (USD) 3-4 X-long shank (USD Note: The hook is dressed or tied upside down to eliminate bottom hang-ups.)

Weight: Options of using leadfree wire wrapped several times around the hook just behind the eye, add cement and cocoon with thread. The fly could also be finished with no weight tied on but fished with a weight on the leader line a few inches above the fly; this allows the hook to be tied in the normal down position.

Thread: Rust or brown

Tail: Wisker fringe formed by gathering and tying a bundle of long rust or root beer colored dyed bucktail hair to make body abdomen, tips are head whiskers, and butts form the fan tail

Underbody: Thorax , brown-green-olive dubbing to build bulk in this area, thorax should be much fuller than abdomen tail section

Eyes: Black plastic dumbbell eyes, or melted heavy mono line beads.

Pincers: Pair of V-clipped brown turkey tail feathers

Antennae: Two brown or black stripped hackle stems

Ribbing: Fine copper wire wound around tail to segment the tail area

Legs: Short section of mottled brown turkey tail quill attached on top of the thorax and will be under the shellback, separate feather barb fibers to mimic legs. (Note the illustration)

Shellback: Dark brown bucktail, tie-in butts behind bead eyes, tips facing hook bend, fold over backwards to hook eye. Tie-down tips at spot between thorax and abdomen

Finish: Cover shellback with several coats of cement or varnish for looks and durability

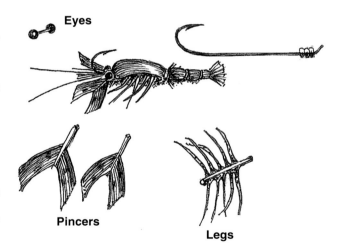

Eyes

Pincers

Legs

Chapter 11: *Gallery of Selected Fly Patterns*

The flies shown here are predominantly tied with deer hair, in one form or another, and will cover almost every flyfishing situation encountered.

ADAMS IRRESISTIBLE

Hook: Dry
Thread: Black or gray
Tail: Deer body hair
Body: Natural deer hair spun and trimmed to shape
Wing: Grizzly hen hackle tips
Hackle: Brown and grizzly mixed

BIG BUG BOMBER

Hook: Dry
Thread: Gray
Body: Spun deer hair trimmed
Rib/Hackle: Palmered grizzly

BLACK GHOST

Hook: Streamer
Thread: Black
Tail: Yellow poly yarn
Body: Black floss
Rib: Silver tinsel
Beard: Yellow poly yarn
Wing: White bucktail

BLACK NOSE DACE

Hook: Streamer
Thread: Black
Tail: Red poly yarn
Body: Flat silver tinsel
Rib: Oval silver tinsel
Underwing: White bucktail
Mid-wing: Black bucktail or black bear
Overwing: Brown bucktail or gray squirrel tail

BLUE SURFACE SPUTTERER

Hook: Salmon or dry fly
Thread: White
Body: Oval gold tinsel
Head and Collar: Dyed blue deer hair spun and trimmed head; untrimmed collar

BULLETHEAD HOPPER

Hook: Streamer
Thread: Yellow
Body: Cream-colored deer hair
Rib: Yellow deer hair
Underwing: Yellow deer hair
Overwing: Pair hen pheasant wing slips
Head: Natural or cream colored bucktail tied bullet style with tips forming the body collar

COFFIN FLY

Hook: Dry
Thread: White
Tail: Three black peccary hairs
Body: White poly yarn and white deer hair dubbing mixture spun onto white thread and wrapped on hook
Rib: White thread counter wrapped over spikey dubbing
Wing: Two equal segments of teal flank
Hackle: Golden badger
Head: Finish with black thread head

COMPARA-DUN

Hook: Dry
Thread: Tan
Body: Fine deer hock hair dubbing
Wing: Deer body hair fanned 180 degrees on top of hook

DADDY LONGLEGS (CRANEFLY)

Hook: Dry
Thread: Brown
Body: Bundled orange-brown bucktail tied on hook shank as extended body
Legs: Cock pheasant-tail fibers, knotted to portray leg joints
Wings: Ginger or cree hackle

DEBRIS CADDIS

Hook: Caddis
Thread: Gray
Body: Spikey deer-hair dubbing
Head: Gray dubbing fur

DEER HAIR BEETLE

Hook: Dry
Thread: Black
Shellback: Black deer hair or bucktail
Underbody: Black fur or poly yarn
Legs: Fold over ends of shellback

DEER HAIR CADDIS

Hook: Dry
Thread: Tan
Body: Tan-brown poly yarn mixed with fine spikey deer hair representing legs
Rib: Fine gold or copper wire
Wing: Light deer hair or bucktail
Head: Butt ends of wing clipped short

DRAGONFLY NYMPH

Hook: Streamer (weighted)
Thread: Black
Body: Brown, green, black and natural bucktail tied onto hook shank broom style
Hackle: Cover butt ends of bucktail with long mallard or woodduck flank feather tied full and swept to rear of hook, separate and mix fibers with bucktail
Head: Thread wrap and finish head as usual

EXTENDED BODY MAYFLY

Hook: Dry
Thread: Tan or brown
Tails: Natural bucktail
Abdomen: Natural bucktail
Thorax: Light brown poly yarn dubbing
Wing: Paired hen pheasant
Hackle: Brown or ginger

FLUTTERING DEER HAIR CADDIS

Hook: Dry
Thread: Brown
Rib: Gold wire
Body: Add a few turns of weight wire at the hook bend. Dub the weight and the hook with olive-tan poly yarn
Wing: Natural deer hair
Antennae: Fox whiskers
Note: The weighted hook butt positions the fly in an egg-dropping attitude just beneath the water surface

FLUTTERING ORANGE STONEFLY

Hook: Streamer
Thread: Orange
Tail: Bown deer hair
Body: Orange poly yarn
Rib: Brown or tan floss
Wing: Long natural deer hair or bucktail topped with shorter dark brown deer hair
Hackle: Tan or ginger trimmed flat on bottom

FOAM HOPPER

Hook: Dry or streamer
Thread: Brown or tan
Body: Light brown closed cell foam
Wing: Deer hair and strands of root beer Krystal Flash
Legs: "Clearwater" colored stretchable polymer

GODDARD CADDIS

Hook: Dry
Thread: Gray or black
Body: Natural deer hair spun and trimmed to shape
Antennae: Two stripped brown hackle stems
Hackle: Brown or chocolate

GOLD RIBBED DEER'S HAIR NYMPH

Hook: Nymph
Thread: Brown
Tail: Natural deer hair
Abdomen: Spikey and loose deer hair for legs, a few drops of cement may be needed
Legs: Picked out from thorax
Wingcase: Brown raffia (Swiss straw) or dark turkey wing slip

GRAY WULFF

Hook: Dry
Thread: Black
Tail: Dark natural deer hair
Body: Gray muskrat or poly dubbing
Wing: Dark natural deer hair
Hackle: Blue dun and grizzly tied full

GREASE LINER

Hook: Dry or salmon
Thread: Tan or brown
Tail: Black deer hair or bucktail tips facing rear
Wing: Same as tail with tips facing forward
Body: Brown poly yarn mixed with fine dark deer hair, cover butt ends of tail and wing, finish with thread head

GREEN DRAKE

Hook: Dry
Thread: Olive
Tail: Long cream or white bucktail
Body: Mixed tan poly yarn and red fox fur
Rib: Heavy dark brown thread or floss
Wing: Two full woodduck flank feathers
Hackle: Grizzly dyed green

GREEN ROCK WORM

Hook: Nymph or caddis
Thread: Green
Body: Fluorescent green bucktail
Rib: Peacock herl
Note: Coat entire fly with tying cement for durability

HAIRY MARY

Hook: Salmon or streamer
Thread: Black
Tag: Oval gold tinsel
Tail: Golden pheasant crest
Body: Black floss
Rib: Oval gold tinsel
Hackle: Bright blue beard
Wing: Natural brown bucktail

IRRESISTIBLE

Hook: Dry
Thread: Tan or brown
Body: Natural deer body hair spun and trimmed to shape
Hackle: Brown and ginger

MICKEY FINN

Hook: Streamer
Thread: Black
Body: Embossed silver tinsel or flat silver tinsel
Rib: Needed only if flat silver tinsel is used for the body then an oval silver rib is necessary
Underwing: Yellow bucktail
Midwing: Red bucktail
Overwing: Yellow bucktail equal in amount to the underwing and midwing combined

SCUD SHRIMP

Hook: Curved shrimp
Thread: Tan or olive
Tail and Body: Tan or olive deer hair
Body and Legs: Dubbed natural or olive dyed fine deer hair (mask)
Shellback: Clear or frosted plastic bag strip or pearl Flashabou
Rib: Tippet material
Note: Substitute orange in place of the olive-colored material (see the illustration on page 32)

LITTLE BROOK TROUT

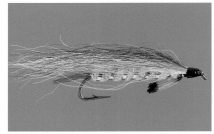

Hook: Streamer
Thread: Black
Tail: Sparse green and brown deer hair
Body: Cream poly yarn or dubbing
Rib: Flat gold tinsel
Beard: Golden pheasant tippets
Wing: Sparse bunches of white bucktail topped by red-orange and green bucktail
Top Cover: Gray squirrel tail

MOHAWK

Hook: Dry
Thread: Brown
Body: Brown deer hair spun on hook, clip the bottom flat and trim top in an 180-degree fan shape
Hackle: Oversized cream or light colored

SILVER MARCH BROWN

Hook: Streamer or wet fly
Thread: Black
Tail: Partridge feather fibers
Body: Flat silver tinsel over a dental floss base
Rib: Oval silver tinsel
Beard Hackle: Turkey hackle fibers
Wing: Brown bucktail topped with black squirrel tail

LITTLE BROWN TROUT II

Hook: Streamer
Thread: Black or brown
Tail: Bronze ringneck breast feather
Rib: Flat gold tinsel or copper wire
Body: Cream fur or poly yarn dubbing
Wing: Sparse equal amounts yellow, red-orange bucktail topped with fox squirrel tail

MUDDLER MINNOW

Hook: Streamer
Thread: Gray or tan
Tail: Mottled turkey wing slips
Body: Gold braid tinsel
Underwing: Gray squirrel tail
Wing: White bucktail covered by a pair of mottled turkey wing sections
Head and Collar: Natural deer hair spun and clipped as shown

SKITTERBUG

Hook: Dry
Thread: Gray
Body: Spun natural deer hair or bucktail, rear spun to the back and front spun forward

TENT WING CADDIS

Hook: Dry
Thread: Spikey, chopped deer-hair dubbing
Wing: Turkey wing quill sections tied-in tent style
Antennae: Fox or raccoon whiskers

USD CLOUSER DEEP MINNOW

Hook: Straight eye
Thread: White
Eyes: Weighted dumbbell eyes
Beard or Belly: Orange and yellow bucktail
Wing or Back: Red bucktail mixed with strands of Krystal Flash
Head: Wrap thread head same color as wing or back

YELLOW HUMPY

Hook: Dry
Thread: Yellow
Tail: Light deer body hair
Underbody: Yellow floss
Overbody: Light deer body hair
Hackle: Mixed ginger and brown

TURKEY SCULPIN

Hook: Streamer
Thread: Brown or tan
Tail: Light speckled turkey quill slip
Body: Flat gold tinsel over dental floss base
Rib: Oval gold tinsel
Hackle: Collar of unclipped deer hair
Underwing: Fox squirrel tail
Wing: Matched light speckled turkey quill slips
Head: Spun dark deer hair and clipped

WARDEN'S WORRY

Hook: Streamer
Thread: Black
Tag: Flat gold tinsel
Tail: Red dyed duck quill slip
Body: Yellow fuzzy poly yarn
Rib: Flat gold tinsel
Throat or Beard: Yellow hackle or yellow deer hair
Wing: Natural bucktail
Head: Black lacquer

YELLOW ENSIGN (STONEFLY)

Hook: Dry
Thread: Black
Tail: Short deer hair
Body: Olive dubbing
Wing: Gray phase deer hair
Sight Aid: Yellow poly yarn
Hackle: Dun

USD CRAYFISH

Hook: Streamer up-side-down
Thread: Rust
Eyes: Black bead chain or plastic dumbbell
Tail: Long rust bucktail
Abdomen: Extended tail material tied on top of brown-olive fur dubbing
Thorax: Spikey brown-olive deer hair dubbed on hook shank over segments of mottled turkey wing quills for legs
Shellback: Dark rust-brown bucktail tied-in mid body and brought forward over thorax
Pincers: V-cut brown turkey quill
Anennae: Two stripped black hackle stems
Head: Pull shellback forward and tie-in with pincers and antennae using figure-8s around the eyes
Finish: Shellback with varnish

Additional Information

This is not a bibliography because that title might give the impression that books have been the sole source of information and instruction on which this "guidebook" has been based. Although I have consulted a good number of books to confirm my information, and to read what others have written about the various fly patterns, the patterns illustrated in this book are based on my own personal experience. Fly variations have and will probably continue to be adapted and changed around the world because most fly tiers are gracious people and freely give their flies, pattern recipes and knowledge to others. There are a number of books, magazines and Internet sites available to a reader who might want to know more about fly-fishing, fly tying and entomology, or the history of these vast subjects.

You should also be aware of another great source of information: the organizations and clubs dedicated to fly fishing. I give credit to Jim Krul regarding our need to support fishing-related organizations and clubs. Jim was the purveyor of English Angling Trappings (EAT) at the time I submitted this book. Since then, EAT has been taken in by the Anglers' Den, 11 Main Street, Pawling, NY 12564. Telephone 1-845-855-5182. The establishment is a full-service outfitter and fly shop for all the fly-fishermen's needs. Along with being on the Catskill Fly Fishing Center and Museum Board of Directors, Jim is the promoter of Flyfishing University in Danbury, CT each year in January.

Jim maintains politics will soon come into play, attacking our fishing habitats, in addition to the body of outsiders who think they know what's best for the fish and the environment. You may have encountered these forces already. Flyfishing-related organizations and clubs are the armor of the fly-fishing community. They offer the participants a place to share experiences, exchange ideas, learn and build programs that positively effect all fly-fishermen. You need to join and be active in a national organization by getting involved on the local club or chapter level. You will be kept aware of the issues and changes that hinder the enjoyment of fly-fishing and what can be done about them to ensure a positive future for ourselves and others.

The Catskill Fly Fishing Center and Museum (CFFC&M) is located right on the famous Catskill fly-fishing waters of the Willowemoc, and near the Beaverkill and Delaware rivers and all their tributary streams. The CFFC&M is not just a regional museum, but is the fly-fishing center for America. Contact CFFC&M, P.O. Box 1295, Livingston Manor, NY 12758. The center stages many exhibits and events throughout the year, it also offers classes in fly-tying and flyfishing-related programs, including rod building, the environment and an extensive youth education program. The center is a place to visit often and if you have some fly fishing collectibles or used items to donate, the youth program will make good use of fly rods, reels, fly lines and whatever.

The Catskill Fly Tyers Guild originated in 1993 to preserve and protect the Catskill fly-tying heritage that enhanced the development of dry-fly fishing in America. Touch base or join the Guild at P.O. Box 0663, Roscoe, NY 12776-0663. Membership fee is $10; you receive a patch, the "Gazette" newsletter, a fly-swap program and first-time members get a copy of the booklet, "Favorite Rivers, Favorite Flies".

The United Fly Tyers is another group offering fly-tying programs, the "Roundtable" newsletter presents old and new fly patterns and recipes, along with the up-coming programs of fly-tying instruction. New members also get a patch and discounts on UFT merchandise. Contact the United Fly Tyers, P.O. Box 2478, Woburn, MA 01888. Yearly membership is $20.

The Theodore Gordon Flyfishers group is a "crow-in-the-tree" organization that keeps a close watch and a warning alert over the traditional fly fishing waters of the Northeast, and supports stream protection and preservation worldwide. The "Gordon's Quill" newsletter will keep you informed of the issues. For more information, write Theodore Gordon Flyfishers, P.O. Box 2345, Grand Central Station, NY 10163 or check their website www.tgf.org. Membership categories and fees range from student to life member.

Please continue your support of the national organizations such as Trout Unlimited and the Federation of Fly Fishers and others by being active in their local clubs and chapters.

Index

About the Artist-Author

JACK PANGBURN is a respected world-class fly tier. He has won many international competitions, including the World Class Open Fly Tying Competition sponsored by Partridge of Redditch, England. Tying competitively since 1990, Jack has won numerous cash awards, prizes and has been included in and contributed to many magazine articles, books and publications. His original patterns and art appear regularly in *Flyfishing & Tying Journal* and he is posted on several web sites. Jack is an Orvis fly-tying instructor, demonstrator and a member of the Federation of Fly Fishermen, the United Fly Tyers, the Catskill Fly Tying Guild and the Catskill Fly Fishing Center, and a long-time member of Trout Unlimited. He is the featured artist in the New York State Department of Environmental Conservation 2002-2004 *Fishing Regulations Guide*.

LEARN MORE ABOUT FISHING WITH THESE BOOKS

TYING EMERGERS: A COMPLETE GUIDE
Jim Schollmeyer and Ted Leeson

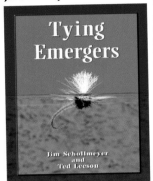

Two of fly-fishing's most well-respected writers collaborate once again, this time discussing emergers. Emergence is itself a behavior, and it puts the tier in a challenging and rather unusual positionænot that of imitating a fixed and recognizable form of the insect, but rather of representing a process. This book shows you how, including: emerger design and materials, basic tying techniques, many specialized tying techniques, fly patterns, and more. When you buy a book by these two authors you know what you will getæup-to-the-minute information, well-written text, and superb photography, Tying Emergers will not let you down. 8 1/2 x 11 inches, 260 pages.

SB: $45.00   ISBN: 1-57188-306-1
SPIRAL HB: $60.00   ISBN: 1-57188-307-X

FEDERATION OF FLY FISHERS FLY PATTERN ENCYCLOPEDIA
Over 1600 of the Best Fly Patterns
Edited by Al & Gretchen Beatty

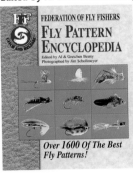

Simply stated, this book is a Federation of Fly Fishers' conclave taken to the next level, a level that allows the reader to enjoy the learning and sharing in the comfort of their own home. The flies, ideas, and techniques shared herein are from the "best of the best" demonstration fly tiers North America has to offer. The tiers are the famous as well as the unknown with one simple characteristic in common; they freely share their knowledge. Many of the unpublished patterns in this book contain materials, tips, tricks, or gems of information never before seen.

As you leaf through these pages, you will get from them just what you would if you spent time in the fly tying area at any FFF function. At such a show, if you dedicate time to observing the individual tiers, you can learn the information, tips, or tricks they are demonstrating. All of this knowledge can be found in *Federation of Fly Fishers Fly Pattern Encyclopedia* so get comfortable and get ready to improve upon your fly tying technique with the help of some of North America's best fly tiers. Full color, 8 1/2 x 11 inches, 232 pages.

SB: $39.95   ISBN: 1-57188-208-1

SPEY FLIES & DEE FLIES: THEIR HISTORY & CONSTRUCTION
John Shewey

The Spey and Aberdeenshire Dee are among the world's great salmon rivers, their storied pools and sea-bright salmon have inspired generations of anglers. Few can fish these rivers, but we all can learn the tying and fishing techniques that made them so famous. Going straight to the source, John found much of the information in this book from the writings of the originators of the Spey and Dee flies. These salmon and steelhead flies are elegant and artfully tied—and they continue to catch fish across the globe. Beautiful photographs enhance this book destined to become a classic. 8 1/2 x 11 inches, 160 pages.

SB: $29.95   ISBN: 1-57188-232-4

MAYFLIES: TOP TO BOTTOM
Shane Stalcup

Shane Stalcup approaches fly-tying with the heart and mind of both a scientist and an artist. His realistic approach to imitating the mayfly is very popular and effective across the West, and can be applied to waters across North America. Mayflies are the most important insects to trout fishermen, and in this book, Shane shares his secrets for tying effective, lifelike mayfly imitations that will bring fly-anglers more trout. Many tying techniques and materials are discussed, *Mayflies: Top to Bottom* is useful to beginner and expert tiers alike. 8 1/2 x 11 inches, 157 pages.

SB: $29.95   ISBN: 1-57188-242-1
Spiral HB: $39.95   ISBN: 1-57188-243-X

CURTIS CREEK MANIFESTO
Sheridan Anderson

Finest beginner fly-fishing guide due to its simple, straightforward approach. It is laced with outstanding humor provided in its hundreds of illustrations. All the practical information you need to know is presented in an extremely delightful way such as rod, reel, fly line and fly selection, casting, reading water, insect knowledge to determine which fly pattern to use, striking and playing fish, leaders and knot tying, fly tying, rod repairs, and many helpful tips. A great, easy-to-understand book. 8 1/2 x 11 inches, 48 pages.

SB: $7.95   ISBN: 0-936608-06-4

HATCH GUIDE FOR NEW ENGLAND STREAMS
Thomas Ames, Jr.

New England's streams, and the insects and fish that inhabit them, have their own unique qualities that support an amazing diversity of insect species from all of the major orders. This book covers: reading water; presentations for New England streams; tackle; night fishing; and more. Ames discusses the natural and its behaviors and the three best flies to imitate it, including proper size and effective techniques. Tom's color photography of the naturals and their imitations is superb! Full color. 4 x 4 inches, 272 pages; insect and fly plates.

SB: $19.95   ISBN: 1-57188-210-3
HB: $29.95   ISBN: 1-57188-220-0

FLY TYING MADE CLEAR AND SIMPLE
Skip Morris

With over 220 color photographs, expert tier show all the techniques you need to know. 73 different materials and 27 tools. Clear, precise advice tells you how to do it step-by-step. Dries, wets, streamers, nymphs, etc., included so that you can tie virtually any pattern. 8 1/2 x 11 inches, 80 pages.

SPIRAL SB: $19.95   ISBN: 1-878175-13-0
SOFTBOUND: $19.95   ISBN: 1-57188-231-6

HOT BASS FLIES: PATTERNS & TACTICS FROM THE EXPERTS
Deke Meyer

Fly-fishing for bass is hotter than ever, and so are the bass flies used to catch them. Combining traditional fur and feathers with modern synthetics, innovative designers have developed bass flies that wiggle and waggle, spin and dart, pop and gurgle, slink and undulate, all of which drive bass wild. In *Hot Bass Flies*, Deke Meyer shares over 200 exceptional bass flies from experts known and unknown alike. 8 1/2 x 11 inches, 136 pages, full-color.

SB: $24.95   ISBN: 1-57188-285-5
SP HB: $39.95   ISBN: 1-57188-286-3

ASK FOR THESE BOOKS AT YOUR LOCAL FLY SHOP OR BOOK STORE.
IF UNAVAILABLE CALL, FAX, OR ORDER ON THE WEB AT WWW.AMATOBOOKS.COM

Frank Amato Publications, Inc. • PO Box 82112 • Portland, Oregon 97282
TOLL FREE 1-800-541-9498 (8-5 Pacific Time) • FAX (503) 653-2766